dove on a barbed wire

deborah steiner-van rooyen

DE**V**ORA

PUBLISHING

NEW YORK◆JERUSALEM◆LONDON

Dove on a Barbed Wire
Published by Devora Publishing Company
Text Copyright © 2010 Deborah Steiner van-Rooyen

A revised, expanded English edition of: *My Grandfather's Brother's Son* (©1987, Eve Press) and the revised Hebrew translation published by Yad Vashem, Jerusalem, Israel © 2007, Hebrew title: *Yonahal Chut Til, Mesa B'Mitzvit Saba.*

COVER DESIGN: Stavros Cosmopulos & www.dvrdesign.com
TYPESETTING, BOOK LAYOUT AND DESIGN: dvrdesign.com
EDITORIAL AND PRODUCTION DIRECTOR: Daniella Barak
EDITOR: Dvora Kiel
FAMILY ALBUM PHOTOGRAPHS: Courtesy of author
FAMILY TREE COMPILATION: www.acertainjustice.com
AUTHOR PHOTOGRAPH: Inger Ronen (2004)

Soft Cover ISBN: 978-1-934440-79-7

Author's book web site: www/doveonabarbedwire.com

E-mail: publisher@devorapublishing.com
Web Site: www. devorapublishing.com

Distributed by:

Urim Publications
POB 52287
Jerusalem 91521, Israel
Tel: 02.679.7633
Fax: 02.679.7634
urim_pub@netvision.net.il

Lambda Publishers, Inc.
527 Empire Blvd.
Brooklyn, NY 11225, USA
Tel: 718.972.5449
Fax: 781.972.6307
mh@ejudaica.com

www.UrimPublications.com

First English edition. Printed in Israel

Dedication

To Rachel Zimmermann Steiner, of blessed memory:
Your watchful mother's eyes can now rest in peace.
Your son, Yonah, is finally home.

TABLE OF CONTENTS

PROLOGUE

In 1969 I decided to go off on a round-the-world adventure rather than spend the coming year as a freshman in college. The afternoon of my departure, my eighty-two-year-old grandfather came by the house to wish me a safe trip. Catching me alone on the front porch, he reached into his pocket, withdrew a faded envelope and, grabbing my arm, pulled me close to him.

"Find my brother's son for me, Deborah," he said in his definitive, patriarchal voice. Stuffing the old envelope into my hand, he pointed to a barely legible return address on the upper left-hand corner. "Find him for me. I have done him an injustice."

A car horn beeped.

My grandfather's shock of white hair, crowned by a black yarmulke, sparkled in the last of the summer day's light. As I ran down the driveway to the waiting car, he remained at the top of the stairs of my parents' house, dominating the porch. My grandfather, Solomon Steiner, stood as he always did — proud and erect — raising a broad, liver-spotted hand that shook slightly from an undefined palsy. His portly bearing was formidable. I looked back up the stairs and waved, then slipped the envelope into the side pocket of my bag. Later I wondered what he meant.

Two months into my journey I found myself in Israel, on a bus to Tiberias, to search for a relative who shared the same last name. The return address on the old envelope contained the barest of information: *Steiner. Kibbutz Ginosar. Israel. 1951.* Eighteen years ago. Somehow I couldn't imagine anyone staying in one place for so long. But my grandfather's words still held a potency I could not easily ignore. Despite my longing to explore the old Roman ruins of Tiberias, my conscience pushed me northward.

By the time I reached the kibbutz, a lovely, lush collective farm spread neatly around the lip of the Sea of Galilee, the sunset was washing the Golan Heights across the lake in a palette of purple and lavender. The bone-dry air of the late September afternoon rustled through the waist-high grass that bordered a dirt road that fed into the kibbutz. Following its direction, I shifted my heavy knapsack onto my back and hiked the quarter mile into the settlement and proceeded to ask for the Steiner family.

Someone directed me to a newly constructed whitewashed cottage with a red-tiled clay roof near the lake's edge. I knocked hesitantly on the door, painted a sterile white, wondering what to say if the person didn't speak English. The door opened. A listless man, elderly in appearance with a complexion the color of paste and a crop of dry, white hair, looked back at me with a blank gaze.

I asked if this was the Steiner family's house.

In halting English, accented in high-pitched, enunciated tones that bore no kinship to the familiar throaty rumble of my grandfather's interpretation of the English language, he said that it was. But the man didn't look like a Steiner to me. Or maybe I didn't want him to be one. His aloof, almost superior manner left me feeling cold and ill at ease. I stood puzzled, thinking he might not understand what I was saying. I forced myself to rally and plastered an encouraging smile on my face. After all, I was about to return to this man his long-lost family.

I held out the fragile envelope. The man inspected the inscription with a farsighted glance, and then shook his head. No, he said, he wasn't the same Steiner. He had never written such a letter. I had made a mistake. I shrugged my shoulders, trying to hide my disappointment.

Understanding the matter closed, I nodded "*Shalom*" and turned to leave.

"Wait," the man called, his voice scratching the air with irritation.

He steadied himself down the steps after me, one slippered foot carefully following another, and pointed across a long field to a group of older, cream-colored cottages rich with clinging ivy and a garden run wild with orange, purple, red, and magenta-colored summer flowers. Perhaps there, he explained, lived the Steiner I was looking for. Yonah Steiner. He was sorry, but his name was Dan.

Yonah Steiner.

I trod across Dan's unplanted lawn, my sandals sinking into the warm, upturned soil. The late afternoon heat shimmered in humid waves over the rustling yellowing reeds along the shoreline of the Kinneret. I felt hot and sticky. With obligation wearing thin on his face, Dan led me brusquely across the path that led toward a row of cottages, then motioned for me to wait at the side of the house by a drooping eucalyptus tree while he knocked on the door of the third house.

A jumble of words in Hebrew came from behind the half-opened screen. I listened to the exchange, wishing that I understood what was being said. Waiting, I watched a group of young fair-haired boys playing ball in the front yard, my eyes fixed on an exquisite little boy with elfin-shaped ears and eyes as translucent green as one of the cat's-eye marbles I collected as a child.

The screen door opened and snapped shut. My eyes jumped back to the porch where a man strode down the three short steps to the grass, passing Dan as if he did not exist. Compared with the elder Steiner, this man looked surprisingly young. I thought at once that this meeting would be another mistake. From the short distance, I could find no resemblance to the portly, aquiline-nosed Steiners that sprinkled the leaves of my family tree. But the man did look familiar in a way, as if I had seen him before but couldn't remember where. As he approached me, his long strides narrowing the distance in seconds,

I searched his face. His high, tanned forehead was framed by close-cropped dark brown hair curling at the edges. He had pointed elf-like ears, a long thin nose that twisted peculiarly to the left, wide thin lips and a solid square jaw. His was a sinewy body, long and lean. He wore an open, white, three-quarter-length-sleeved shirt unbuttoned to his ribs, and kibbutz-issued shorts. His feet were shoeless. I suspected he must be in his mid-forties, yet he showed no sign of developing the prosperous Steiner paunch. But when he gripped my hand with a powerful handshake that nearly paralyzed me, I knew I had found him. I would recognize that stubborn, Steiner, hard-driven force anywhere in the world.

"*Solomon?*"[1]

The word crept from his lips, its sound throaty, guttural. His small green eyes creased and a hundred lines radiated from both corners in sharp diagonals cutting through his cheeks, bending freckles in their path.

I nodded my head. He knew my grandfather! Yonah gripped my hands again, digging his fingers into my skin. I looked down, aware that his grasp was hurting me, when my eyes fell on a blue and red tattoo on his forearm that swirled into a crude illustration of a bird with wings spread in flight, caught within a flower and a red sun. I felt a strange repulsion. *How could someone from my family tattoo himself?* I thought. I looked down again at the design, wondering how I would ever extricate myself from his grip, and noticed a second tattoo engraved in the crook of his other arm. I was unable to stop myself from staring, and my eyes riveted themselves to the inky-blue tattooed face of a girl with short, solid-blue hair and blue bangs, which lay inside a flat design against his skin. And then I saw, against the flesh of his inner arm, camouflaged within a halo of blue inky flowers and swirls, the number.

I must have flinched because he let go of my hands.

I looked away, embarrassed that I had seen something I shouldn't have. A secret. An ugly secret. Painfully conscious of my discovery, I looked up at this man's face, reading his features with new understanding. His face, the skin pulled tight around the sharp bones of his cheeks, skull-like, had the unmistakable markings of a man who had seen hunger and death. Now I knew why he looked familiar. I had seen his photograph before in my history books when I read about Germany and the war and the Nazis. When I read about the victims of the concentration camps.

My eyes found their way to his arm again. I stared at the indigo blue letters above his right wrist — thin, needle-sharp letters that engraved the letters "KL" into his skin. I had never seen that before in my life, and I felt ashamed that I never knew about his suffering until now. My own family.

Yonah Steiner was studying my face when I looked at him again. There were small, almost indistinguishable tears in the corners of his eyes. I will never forget how much pain I felt for him at that moment and how much I didn't understand. I wanted to say something. But while we shared a common set of genes, a common heritage, we couldn't exchange the simplest of words. Yonah spoke no English. I knew no Hebrew. I felt frustrated, confused, and suddenly acutely embarrassed by my silver-spooned American origins. There were so many things I wanted to know right then. How could it be that I slumbered comfortably in a bed in suburban New Jersey for eighteen years while this other member of my family knew only terror? How did this man, this one Steiner, come to survive Hitler and end up in Israel? What happened to this Yonah Steiner during the war? What happened to all the Steiners? Why had I never asked about it before? Why was I never told?

"Please find my brother's son," my grandfather had asked.

I had found my grandfather's brother's son. But it wasn't enough. I had to know more. Why did my grandfather carry around a guilty secret for so many years? Who was this man named Yonah Steiner and what did he have to do with me?

I stayed on Kibbutz Ginosar for over a year, working as a volunteer, and later remained in Israel for another three years. Yonah accepted me into his family as if I were his own daughter. Over a period of six months I learned Hebrew because Yonah wouldn't speak to me in any other language. No one spoke to him in any language other than Hebrew when he first came to Palestine in 1947, Yonah explained through a translator that first afternoon. I would learn Hebrew by the same method.

Yonah kept his word and I learned the language. And when I learned the language, I learned about my family. I learned the story of the destruction of the Steiner family in Europe and of the survival of my grandfather's brother's son. One survivor in Israel out of my grandfather's nine brothers and sisters; their multitudes of children, numbering over seventy-five; and my great-grandparents, Aharon and Sarah Steiner, each and every one of them now burnt offerings to a seemingly deaf God.

Yonah shared his history with me; his story of our family's origins, our once-upon-a-time life before the Nazis altered the world and burned the branches of our family tree. That story, along with his survival in and escapes from five separate concentration camps, appears on the following pages. I have spent over a year translating the tapes of his story from Hebrew into English.[2] At first I transcribed Yonah's interview for our Israeli and American family record, for Yonah's sons, who never knew their own father's past. Then I came to understand that Yonah's story needed to be heard by everyone's family because it is, indeed, a story of universal value, a story of heroism, survival, determination, and courage.

Come meet my grandfather's brother's son.

PART I:
YONAH

CHAPTER ONE: Gromnik

Once upon a time, long before you were born, long before your father or I was conceived, the Steiners had their beginnings as minor landowners, horse traders, and cattlemen in Germany. Every few decades, however, some restless ancestor, scratching the itch of his nomadic blood, drifted eastward from Germany in search of further prosperity, which is how my grandparents and your great-grandparents came to settle in the southern regions of the Austrian Empire, which later became Galicia, Poland, around the time of the First World War.

I was born in Gromnik, a little farming town in the southeast of the province of Tarnowa,[3] right at home in my mother's bed. But then all of us were born at home in those days. Imagine going to a hospital for something so natural! We lived in a large, comfortable farmhouse with a red tile roof that my father had built a few kilometers outside of town. It was a solid house of rough wood with three sleeping chambers and a large living room/kitchen area with a hard stone floor. Papa didn't believe in climbing stairs. He used to say he worked hard enough in the fields, so our house grew out rather than up. My father had put in one long window in the main room that looked out over the fields, but the rest of the walls were built of layered logs and mud to keep out the cold.

During the long winters a smoking wood-burning stove with blue ceramic tiles warmed our toes and our mugs of hot milk. Those blue tiles were not just any ordinary tiles, mind you. My mother had picked each and every one from the handiwork of a local artisan. When I was a little boy, I remember, I counted the artfully painted flowers and birds on the tiles as I curled up in front of the stove. When

I finished I would roll over and watch the snowflakes wander past the big window onto the fields, and I'd daydream. Beyond that window and at the edge of the field grew a huge forest, deep with tall pine trees — a good place to hide when you were a small boy and supposed to be helping your father stack the hay or sitting on a stiff wooden stool at school.

Our farm sat on a great tract of land my father bought after he returned from four years' imprisonment as a Polish soldier in Russia. He built himself a house, and after ten childless years of marriage finally produced four sons, one after another. And he grew content. But because of all of this wealth and comfort, he didn't want to leave any of it behind when he should have done so. My stubborn father, Simon[4] Steiner — his property had more value to him than his survival or the survival of his family.

Once we were a big family. My eldest brothers, twins named Willi and Rudi,[5] were born in 1922. Poldek came in 1924, and I, Yonah, (or *Jonas* as it was written in Polish) was the last to follow in 1926. Four boys after ten years of marriage was quite an achievement. My father was proud, rightly so, although God knows, we created enough trouble around the farm to make him change his mind more than once.

Our life at home was happy. I don't remember if we suffered from the lack of anything, that is, if we were well off or not well off. There was always plenty of food on the table, and warm, clean clothes on our backs. Even if you had money in those days, you would never throw it around or show it off. You would save it for the harder days that for a farmer would always come, if not that year, then the following one when too little or too much rain fell. No, we weren't poor. Maybe by today's standards we might have been, but, well, life was different then.

My father grew a bit of everything: nuts, wheat, potatoes, vegetables. We traded cattle and we also raised horses, which interested me more than what was growing under the ground. My horse was a big, lumbering, gray mare with black spots. I called her Biala after the river that bordered our farm. I rode Biala through the fields to the Polish grammar school in town everyday. She was a good horse. I'd leave her in front of the schoolhouse, feed her an apple and, when school let out at noontime, find her still waiting for me to hop on her back and gallop down the main road to the *cheder*, our Jewish school, where I had been "persuaded" by the back of my father's hand to study Hebrew and the Talmud until late afternoon.

Until my seventh birthday, which made me an official candidate for the school room, I spent the days playing outside in the fields or following my father as he made his rounds about the farm, putting his nose here and there, checking on the laborers who worked for him.

My father was a tall, thin man with dark brown hair that stood up from his head like the bristles on a brush. I remember how the workers would stare at Papa, their eyes wide with jealousy. When he passed, they would complain, "Look how much property this Jew has. He has this and he has that. And we, what have we got?"

Their voices nettled me. I'll never forget them. We were Jews, after all, and they were peasants beholden to a Jew. My father was a good man, and he was good and fair to his workers. But it didn't matter. In the end they were Poles, and Poland was a nation of people who did not tolerate outsiders. The fact that my father didn't run a religious household and that we wore common clothes and spoke Polish at home didn't matter to them. We were Jews. That branded us in their eyes and stirred their envy and animosity.

In truth, it was my mother who persisted in maintaining a traditional Jewish home. Because of her, we kept a kosher table, didn't mix milk with meat, never ate pork, cleaned out the *hametz* (leavened food) on Passover and were forced to go to cheder after school and the synagogue on the Sabbath.

My mother, Rachel, came from the Zimmermann family of

Gribow, a little town south of Gromnik. She was a very beautiful woman with raven-black hair that was the envy of the neighborhood. She never hid her hair behind a kerchief like the Orthodox women. Instead, almost to prove her independence, she kept her hair thick and shiny, combed down her back to her waist. Sometimes on the Sabbath she would plait her hair into a long black braid. My mother was a large-boned woman, proud and straight-backed, and seemed taller to me than my father. She had a delicate face with full red lips and round white teeth. Perfect teeth. But, in thinking back forty years, I can still see her eyes. That's what I remember most — their blueness; it would warm you to her, protect you...a mother's eyes. My mother, Rachel Zimmermann Steiner, was thirty-five when I was born and she was forty-seven when she was murdered. To me, she will always remain as I remember her, young, strong, and beautiful.

Unfortunately, I never really knew my mother's family. They were a long and bumpy three-day cart ride away. But the Steiners, my father's family, were a large-numbered clan who lived in and around our province. Our family connections were fierce and loyal.

Our farm lay half a kilometer down the road from the farm of your great-grandparents, my grandfather Aharon and my grandmother Sarah. We spent every Sabbath with them, along with a multitude of other cousins. Aunts, uncles, cousins — it seemed there was always a tribe of relatives visiting. Each of Grandpa Aharon's nine children, my uncles and aunts, also had as many children. My brothers and I went to school with my father's sister Ciarna's[6] and her husband, Uncle Hersch Mannsdorf's, seven children: Esther, Malka, Gita, Franka, and Mina, and two sons, Yosef and Natan. They lived right next door to us on the farm. And when Uncle Herschel Steiner, my father's eldest brother, and his wife, Aunt Dacha, came to visit from their house next to the cemetery in the village center, there wasn't any place to sit at the table, there were so many children. Not to mention that the Steiners continued to marry daughters and sons of families from within the nearby towns and villages of Tuchow, Choinik, Zawada and Olszowa/Bresko. There were Schlangers, Zorns, Zimmermanns, Goldmans, Gehlers, Mannsdorfs, and Wildsteins, and we were all related in one way or another. It is hard to imagine that from such a large family in Europe, only two of us survived.

Despite the legions of siblings and their progeny, the patriarchy fell without question to Grandpa Aharon, who ruled over us with his mahogany cane and domineering will. He was a handsome man and, as I recall, was a bit thinner and taller than my father. Grandpa Aharon kept a long, curly beard and looked very forbidding. Unlike my father, he spoke sternly and always seemed angry with one or another of his sons. No one, you see, except my father and my father's sister Ciarna, wanted to stay behind in the country and work the farm. My uncles preferred to make their way in the city. Of Grandpa Aharon's nine children, six were sons — the first was Herschel, who lived in the town of Gromnik and opened a tannery near the Polish grammar school and next to the cemetery. His name and business were listed in the 1939 Polish Yellow Pages because he had the first telephone in the village. He married Dacha Wildenstein and they had nine children, most of whom were ahead of me in school. Then came Uncle Arieh, who blinded himself by pouring urine in his eye to keep out of the Austrian army (although I think the story told was that he was blinded by a gang of Polish thugs). Eventually he ran off to become a *hasid* in Bobov and when he visited, I thought he was trying to disguise himself by wearing a great fur-lined *streimel* on his head and a silk, striped *hapek* (long jacket). My father Simche, or Simon as he was known, came third; then your grandfather Solomon, who made his way to America the minute he was old enough to run off; followed by a brother David, who was gassed in World War I and never really recovered. He died in 1928 soon after. At the tail end, born exactly as the century turned in 1900, came the youngest son, Sidney, who I heard soon followed your grandfather to the States when he was seventeen.

And there were three Steiner daughters: Aunt Fradl (Frajah), whose husband was killed in the woods behind the house in front of her eyes by a gang of anti-Semites and was then sent to stay with your grandfather Solomon in the States; and Aunt Chana (Annie), also brought to the States by your grandfather. Only Aunt Ciarna stayed behind because she fell in love with a scoundrel named Hersch Mannsdorf, a neer-do-well the family was forever bailing out of scrapes with the law when he'd cook up some scheme to make money that never came to anything but trouble. As I told you, Aunt Ciarna and Uncle Hersch lived in the log house next to Grandpa Aharon and Grandma Sarah and added another nine children to the family. They used to sell clothing and small dry goods from their front cabin window to those who passed by on the main road.

Grandpa Aharon's fourth adult son, Solomon (your grandfather and my father's next-younger brother), was the first to leave Poland for America. I think it happened before World War I so he could escape the Austrian army draft. Until Uncle Solomon visited us in 1932, I never knew him. But we heard about him plenty. Every Sabbath, Grandpa Aharon lorded over us with his cane waving in the air when he read Uncle Solomon's letters, which told only and always about his good fortune in America. More than a few times your Grandpa Solomon would try to get the whole family to move there. But Grandpa Aharon was as stubborn as he was content to stay in Poland.

"What would I do in America?" he would demand as he slammed his fist on the table, making the wine glasses jump.

Unfortunately, my own father resembled his father in will. He was a true Steiner, stubborn and proud, a man whose word was the last word and law. It was also his end.

So you see, before the Nazis came, I had a pleasant childhood, not because of Poland, but because of our home. Look, we were four boys on one huge farm. What could be better than that? We would play together out in the fields, in the woods, up in the hayloft in the barn, out with the field hands. From time to time, of course, we thought nothing of giving each other a good beating, especially at night when we had to sleep in the same bed. Then we would argue plenty. Feathers would fly from pillows that grew thinner each night. But most of the arguments were settled by a good strong punch and then the guilty party would repent and we would be friends again.

My twin brothers were not identical. Wolf, or Willi as we called him, was tall. He resembled my mother and inherited her black, wavy hair that he swept back from his forehead in a kind of pompadour that was the style of the day. I lived in awe of Willi. He was a handsome boy and very bright. Rudi, his twin, stood a little shorter, a little rounder. He had a more Steiner-looking face, like Papa, with the thicker nose and stockier build. Poldek looked more like Rudi and I think I take after Grandpa Aharon, or maybe the resemblance was closer to my mother's eldest brother, Jonas (Yonah) Zimmermann, in whose memory I was named.

I must say being the youngest had its advantages.

Usually when we got into trouble, which we managed to do with some frequency, the belt would meet my behind last. Well, maybe that's not completely accurate.

I won't easily forget one potato harvest when Willi, Rudi, Poldek and I went out to the fields for our own private roasting party. We made a terrific fire, threw the potatoes into the coals and, when they were toasted, stuffed ourselves full and waddled back home in time for dinner. Only, before we left, we forgot to put out the fire. Nearly half of my father's fields burned down because of us. That time, my father's belt did not defer to age. We all caught a hiding. We couldn't sit down for a good week. I didn't blame my father for his temper. We gave him enough to worry about.

A train passed by not too far from our house. A metal guardrail divided the tracks from a road that crossed it at that junction and automatically lowered itself whenever a train passed. One afternoon we were playing on the guardrail and just as a train hooted its whistle from around the bend, Willi jumped up and grabbed the metal armature to stop it from lowering. By accident, his fingers became twisted in the wheel and chain mechanism. Willi fell down across the tracks along with the lowering guardrail, his two fingers locked inside the meshing cogs. Poldek and I tore up to the house and found our father, who raced back with us to the tracks and managed to saw the chain free from Willi's fingers seconds before the train flew by. From then on, Willi's left index and middle fingers were useless and hung limply down on his palm. Papa didn't beat us then, although we probably deserved it. Anyway, all four of us learned our lesson that day. We didn't need Papa's strap.

I can tell you that as I grew older, Papa's belt found its way to my bottom more than to my brothers'. For example, there were plenty of days when I just didn't manage to get to school. There were too many other diversions along the way — ice-skating on the lakes, skiing through the woods, riding Biala out to the fields.

At the end of most weeks, Papa would get a notice from the principal asking why his son hadn't been in school that week. My poor teacher couldn't understand me. She had taught my older brothers, who were good students, diligent and quick at their lessons. I was a different story, full of chutzpah, a roughneck with a tough mouth. By second grade I had earned quite a reputation for throwing a good fight, which always appealed to me more than sitting still in class. But I never fought without a just cause.

One winter in the third grade, a husky village boy from the next grade ambushed me during recess as I skied by through the field.

"Get out of here, Jew," he sneered, jumping out at me from behind a tree.

I stopped, turned around and grabbed his neck, then punched him straight in the face. Mind you, I wasn't such a small boy. I was big and strong for my age. Strong enough that I belted him and made him bleed in five different places. I left him behind and skied back to school. Later that afternoon, the same boy came into my class hand in hand with the principal, complaining that I had beaten him. The principal ignored my side of the story and punished me with two extra hours at the blackboard.

But it wasn't over.

My parents were called into the office. My father stood sternly in front of the principal. He did not defend me. Only later as we walked home, he said, "Yonah, if you have to beat someone, hit him as hard as you can. Just don't leave any marks." My father's fingers pressed into my shoulder relaying his message. "And, if you see there is going to be a fight with someone," he added, "hit him before he hits you, so he will be afraid, so he will be the one to go home and complain to his parents that he was licked. From you, I never want to hear it."

This lecture took place a few years before things got very bad for us. But I remember it, maybe because I sensed the tone as a sign of things to come, or maybe because my father's voice held a warning. When my report card came out at the end of the sixth year, I was given a bad mark on my behavior. They wouldn't let me pass to the next class. I wasn't your best student either. Nevertheless, I proved a force to be reckoned with. It didn't take long before the Polish boys learned to watch out when I walked in. Being the youngest in my family didn't mean I was the weakest. I never asked my brothers to help me when I got into trouble. In fact, at school, the other boys would run to tell them, "Your brother Yonah is beating up so-and-so." I looked at it this way: my brothers were good students and I was a good fighter. Everyone has to have some area of expertise.

The fact was, and remains until this day, I was never frightened of anybody.

But I had a Jewish friend who was.

Mendel Gehler's family owned the prosperous Slivovitz plum brandy factory in Gromnik. Their house stood at the side of the bridge in the center of the village. The youngest of three boys, Mendel was a weak and cowardly little fellow who shared my desk at school. When I wasn't around to protect him, he used to get beaten up.

During a school trip to the forest to celebrate a Polish national holiday, two big boys dragged little Mendel off into the woods and beat him with sticks, branches, and their fists — all because he was a typical Jewish weakling. They broke his two front teeth, bloodied his nose, and gave him one hell of a black eye. He was only nine years old.

There were so many children running about and only one teacher per class, so no one knew about or heard the scuffle. I knew because Mendel came crying to me. First I took him down to the river and washed his face. Then I went to the teacher to complain about the beating. She said she would look into it.

By the time we got to his home, his eye was black and blue and his cheeks were puffy. When his mother saw him, she broke down and wept. Seeing her cry cut right through to my heart. To this day, I can't see a child crying or bear a woman's tears. I just can't take it. I become crazy from the hurt.

When I left Mendel's house, I thought and thought about how to catch those two *mamzerim.*[7] By luck, I found them the following Sunday in Gromnik coming out of the tobacco shop. Mendel and I had just come from the Jewish school and I dragged him to face his tormentors.

"So, Jew," the Polish boy taunted, "What do you want?"

The Pole turned and circled us several times. And I circled him.

Then I stopped and asked, "Do you remember this little boy?" He answered by slamming his fist into my face. Mendel squirmed under my hand in fear and ran off.

I stayed and fought.

I came home with two swollen eyes, but the Polish boy went home with ten broken fingers.

From that day on, life for me in school became a lesson in survival. Or more like a small-scale war between the local Polish boys and me. They would come at me from the alleys or from behind the school-yard. Rocks flew like bullets.

Eventually a teacher interrupted one of our scuffles and dragged us into the office to find out what was going on. When the reason came out, she dropped the matter. I didn't care anyway, because the Polish boys had received a licking that would last them for a long while, and I had become a hero to my Jewish classmates. Their bodyguard. Wher-ever I went, the other Jewish boys would walk behind me. And so, when the Polish boys saw me coming they would leave us alone.

You've asked me why we stayed then, knowing how the Poles hated us. But I'll tell you, it was the same state of affairs we had lived with for centuries. Besides, where were we to go? It was only when your grand-father Solomon came to visit us from America that the subject of leav-ing Poland was ever discussed. Funny, I must have been no older than six years, but I still remember the visit.

It was *Pesach* (Passover). Grandma Sarah prepared a huge Seder and invited every member of the Steiner family. The number of cousins, uncles, aunts, and grandchildren was enormous. How we all fit around the long oak table at Grandpa Aharon's house amazes me to this day. Grandma Sarah Zorn Steiner, a great organizer, had us little ones working for days before Solomon's arrival, polishing the candle-sticks, sweeping out the crumbs of the hametz, turning the house into a grand welcome for this great son of hers.

When the evening finally came, I can recollect only one image — your grandpa smoking a fat cigar, wearing a top hat and richly tai-lored suit with a gold watch fob, carrying a polished walking stick. He looked very important as he sat in the honored place to the right of his father. Grandpa Aharon's thin chest expanded with pride at his son from America. It was as if a star had fallen on him.

After Uncle Solomon's visit and subsequent departure,

Grandpa Aharon bragged about him for months. I haven't seen your grandfather since, but I cannot forget him.

You might wonder why we didn't pack our bags right then and head for America. Your grandfather Solomon begged his parents to come. He warned them. But you must try to understand that the Steiner family of Austria/Poland was basically a comfortable family. We had land, and therefore neither the will nor the need to find a better place to live.

I remember later, after Uncle Solomon's visit and throughout the rough years in school, my mother would often say to my father, "Simon, we must sell our land and go to Palestine. Now is the time, before things get worse."

Her words stuck in my head. I suppose I carried them with me all the years through the camps and the war, so when I learned that our home and our family had been forever destroyed, I thought immediately of going to Palestine, as my mother had wanted.

Why Palestine, I didn't know. We were not a Zionist family. Oh, my father would send money to Israel but that was about the extent of his involvement. Yet my mother always believed that Palestine was where we should be. But until 1937 there was no strong motivation to move, and by 1938 it was too late.

In 1937 there were massive demonstrations and riots against the Jews. The political and social atmosphere grew tense. In the late evenings when we were supposed to be sleeping, I would hear my parents discuss what they should do. My mother kept begging Papa to sell the farm and leave Poland. My father, hoping things would get better, didn't want to lose all that he had worked for and told her to wait and see what developed.

In 1938 the Polish police renewed their attacks on us. I didn't pay much attention to what was going on, but I heard they had burned the synagogues and soon afterward our religious school was closed, which only meant more free time for me.

In 1939 Germany went to war against Poland and within two weeks occupied the country. I was studying at the Polish grammar school in Gromnik and had just reentered the sixth grade, which I was forced to repeat due to my bad behavior. I had to walk to school now because the Germans had taken Biala, our farm horses, and our cattle — almost everything. My father still held on, believing the situation was only temporary and tried to get by without the horses and the cattle.

And then one afternoon, they took me.

The last time I saw my brothers Willi, Rudi, and Poldek, they were working near home. Their schools had been shut down since the beginning of the war. Only my school, the Polish grammar, was still open. The mood at home grew tense, a pressure underlined with fear. As I said, I was aware of the situation but didn't pay much attention to it. My mother, in an attempt to maintain a normal atmosphere, kept sending me off to school.

As usual that last morning, she tucked in my shirt, smoothed down my collar and kissed me goodbye.

The last thing my mother said was, "Yonah, be careful." That was all.

With those words, I began my last walk to school.

CHAPTER TWO: Pustkow

It was a day late in the autumn, I believe, because the weather already had a slight chill to it. Most of the leaves had fallen from the trees, leaving their bark raw and black against a gray, cloudy sky.

And so the nightmare began.

Like any other day, with school over by noon, I crossed through the village and headed for the small bridge that passed over the Biala River and marked the main road from Gromnik north to Tuchow or west to Choinik. Home was only a short, two-kilometer[8] walk from there. My stomach rattled. I was hungry for lunch. As I approached the bridge, I looked up and saw a line of army lorries surrounded by a group of German SS soldiers and a crowd of Poles. The trucks were positioned diagonally across the bridge, blocking all outgoing traffic on the road. I felt no sense of apprehension, perhaps only curiosity, and made my way toward them.

As I stepped onto the bridge, a man standing at the side of the road pointed at me with an agitated finger. I recognized him as a local merchant my father did business with and almost raised my arm to wave a hello when I heard him shout out to the soldiers, *"Jeszcze jeden Zyd*!" *"*(There's another Jew!)"

It all happened so fast.

The Germans raised their weapons and ordered me directly into the back of the truck. I climbed in without question while the Poles stood by and shouted, "Bravo!" Why didn't I run away? Why didn't I fight? What was a thirteen-year-old boy to do against a troop of SS with machine guns? What did I understand? At the time, I didn't consider the situation as serious. I had heard the Poles were being sent to help the Germans with the war effort. Perhaps my youth and ignorance kept me from feeling fear, and perhaps, looking back, it was what also kept me alive.

I scrambled into the open truck and joined a dozen men who were sitting silently in the back of the lorry. Because they looked much older to me, probably young men in their late teens or early twenties, I assumed they knew what was going on. So it did not occur to me to jump off or try to escape. It surprised me only that the Germans had chosen me for their work needs. I suppose I looked much older than I actually was. Even though I had only just passed my thirteenth birthday, I was big, strong, and tall for my age.

At any rate, I didn't think we would be going far, and certainly would not be away longer than a few days. I worried only that my mother and father would not know where I was. Then I saw a neighbor pass by on the road. I yelled out to him from the truck hoping he would run and tell my parents what had happened. After a few more men were added to our group, the truck sped off.

It grew darker and the hours passed. I knew we were being taken a long way from home. It was then that I began to be concerned. No one spoke. No one knew anyone else. We each sat wrapped in our own thoughts and waited...for what, we didn't know and could not even begin to imagine.

After driving about five hours deep into the night, we finally came to a Polish army base. By now I began to realize that it wasn't going to be exactly as I had expected. My thoughts began to change. I wondered what was going to happen to us. I wasn't afraid. I only worried how my parents would know where I was. I didn't want my mother to become upset.

When we arrived at the camp, the soldiers ordered us off the truck so quickly that I left my school bag behind. The Germans went through our pockets and took whatever money or small change we had, then separated all of us — one here, another there — and sent us off to different barracks.

My barrack was already crowded with a few hundred men. I found a corner and sat down, feeling hungry and very cold, and listened to the other men talk about digging ditches for the Germans. The room was bare. There were no windows, no doors. The floor was the cold, damp earth, the walls, planks of rotting, wet wood. I kept to myself, huddled against the wall. It was a freezing night. We had no beds, no blankets. I tightened my arms around my thin fall jacket and fell asleep.

In the morning, the Germans pounded on the walls and called us outside for a head count. It was then I had my first shock. I saw a contingent of about 5,000 bedraggled men standing in an enormous yard. I looked at those poor people, row after row of terribly suffering, miserable, and dirty men. My own stomach howled with hunger and knotted with pain and apprehension. I had never seen such a sight and the massive suffering left me tremendously depressed. I didn't know what to think. I didn't have anyone to ask what was going on. Each man was closed within himself. No one knew what awaited him.

I studied the men in the rows and wondered how they came to be dressed in such dirty clothing that looked more like rags, mud-splattered and torn civilian dress. Some were dressed in Polish army uniforms; many of the men were barefoot even though there was snow on the ground.

How can I tell you how I felt? I couldn't understand what was happening, what would happen the next day or the day after that. And when I asked, no one knew. I felt as if I were in a vacuum of darkness.

Still, I felt no fear.

The head count lasted for about three quarters of an hour. Afterwards, the soldiers separated us into groups and we went off to work.

There were one hundred men to each unit. We walked out to a large field and began to dig ditches. Long, deep ditches. The cold ripped through my clothing and then rain fell on us, turning into a wet snow. Ours was not work, it was punishment. The soldiers beat us if we didn't do what they wanted or didn't do it fast enough.

The first day I managed to escape their beatings, but I watched in horror as the Germans moved among us and struck at the men with their rifle butts if they slowed their pace. The foremen were even more fearsome than the Germans. Organized from among the Polish prisoners, the foremen called themselves "kapos." They carried clubs and beat us without hesitation if we faltered or rested.

Fifteen men from my group had either been killed or died from the cold or starvation that first day. I had never seen a dead person in my life. My stomach rebelled. I felt nausea creeping into my throat. I wanted to throw up, but I had an empty stomach. You watched people being beaten or killed and you could do nothing to help. It was forbidden to move from your place. All I thought was, *Why were there so many injured, so many dead people here? What was going on?*

When we came back to the camp it was already seven o'clock in the evening. We had been out since six that morning. Again we stood outside in the cold for a head count; this time they counted both the living and the dead whom we had dragged back from the fields with us. By the time we returned to our barracks, it was long after seven and we still hadn't eaten. Still no one spoke. New people were continually being mixed in with the old timers — a disorienting effect. I don't think it's possible to describe a day like that. The weaker prisoners did not survive the day. I was stronger, so it seemed, because I lived. I tried not to think of home because I didn't know what to think. I only felt cold and hungry.

That night we each received half a can of cold soup and some potatoes. I gobbled down the food, and, completely exhausted and depressed, fell right asleep.

It had been a very cold night. In the morning, when the kapo came to the block, shouting us awake, I saw that one half of our group didn't get up. At the roll call, I watched the dead being hauled out to be counted and then carted off to one of the trenches we had dug just the day before.

The camp's name was Pustkow.[9] It was located somewhere near Debica, north of our province. Ours was a slave labor camp, not a concentration camp as they later came to be known. People were not being systematically murdered at that time, just used for their labor until they had no strength left. Then they were killed or they died from exhaustion, dysentery, hunger. As the days went by, fewer and fewer people survived. I heard that Polish soldiers were imprisoned on the other side of the camp, but we were not allowed to mix with them. Our situation seemed hopeless and doomed.

I spent four months at Pustkow.

Somehow I stayed alive.

In the middle of this period, I remember marching to a railroad station to unload coal from freight trains to put onto lorries for the Germans. There, I met a Polish soldier prisoner. We worked side by side, this soldier and I, unloading the sooty, black coal. We started to talk. He told me he wanted to escape. The thought had never occurred to me in a serious way, as a serious possibility. I looked at him as if he were mad. At the time it was all talk, because nothing happened. Not then.

By the end of the day we had been separated, but the idea of escape stayed with me. You see, the situation at the camp had become desperate. It was a true Hell. There were no beds, no water. Food was scarce. When you went to the latrines, you went two at a time, and when you returned, you had to return in twos even if your partner had died along the way. The Germans were very clever in devising this buddy system. It defeated any attempts at escape and guaranteed that each man would look after his partner if he wanted to avoid a beating.

In the entire four months, we never showered. And the food had degenerated into a cup of hot water with a little color in the morning and one loaf of bread that had to be divided among twenty men.

Through all these days, the thirteen-year-old boy who filed out to the fields, dug ditches, unloaded coal, watched the dead carried away, fended off blows — that boy was not me. The carefree, happy youngster from a safe, comfortable farm in Gromnik had gone, and in his place there grew an empty soul who moved and survived like a machine.

It took a good two months before I woke up to what was happening around me. This wake-up call came about one day when I went off with my partner to work digging trenches under the bridge below the railroad station. On the bridge stood a few German soldiers holding rifles. They watched us, sometimes silently, sometimes shouting at us to hurry, to move faster. They were a constant presence, and our masters. I needed to relieve myself. In order to do so, I first had to ask permission. But remember, if you go, your partner goes too. So, permission granted, my work partner and I moved out from under the bridge. I squatted against a bush.

Suddenly I heard a rifle shot. My neck burned and I felt something hot on my back. I got up quickly and looked around to grab my partner to run for cover. I couldn't move without him. But as I turned, I saw that a bullet had hit him between the eyes and he stared blankly up at me. I looked up to the bridge and saw the Germans laughing.

I couldn't go back to work in the trench without my partner, so I carried him on my shoulders and dragged him back under the bridge. One of the German guards followed me from the bridge. He looked down at the dead man and said, "*Was ist das?*"

I didn't know how to answer. He knew what had happened. He had shot my partner himself.

I mumbled something about him getting in the way of a bullet. The German shrugged his shoulders, kicked the corpse and went back to his station.

A prisoner who stood behind me said there was blood gushing down my neck. Until he mentioned it, I hadn't felt anything. When I turned my head to look behind me, I saw the back of my shirt was full of blood. I quickly located a bullet hole in my neck. The bullet that had felled my partner had passed grazed through the corner of my neck. I ripped off part of my shirt and wrapped it around my throat.

From that day, I saw this was not a game and that in order to survive, I had to use my wits and save my strength. I had to consciously think about how I could continue without breaking down. I thought only of how to get from one day to another. Again I began to think about finding a way to escape. Each day in camp seemed like a year, even more.

From that moment on, I was determined to find a way out.

CHAPTER THREE: The First Escape

It came without warning on a day of foul, heavy rain and chilling cold, with fields so muddy that it was impossible for us to work. After our head count, the Germans ordered us to do our laundry and wash. I wasn't about to do any laundry. Hundreds of prisoners were moving all around the camp, washing and talking. So I went off looking, searching, always searching for a way out.

I remembered the Polish soldier-prisoner from the railway station who had spoken to me of escape, and I decided to look for him. A low barbed-wire fence separated his Polish Army work camp from ours. I jumped over it and found him sitting with a group of men on the front stoop of their barracks. We started to talk about why we weren't working, and about the war, and the conditions in the camp.

The soldier pulled me aside and asked if I was ready to escape.

"I'm ready any time you say," I told him.

No one asked, no one noticed that I was a thirteen-year-old boy. No one cared that I was about to make an escape with a twenty-five-year-old soldier. No one asked questions like that. We never knew anyone else's name — we didn't need to know. We just took each other at face value, based on a barbed wire of trust. Escape agreed upon, we now had to find a way out.

We all knew the guard around the camp was heavy. The German SS had us surrounded by dogs, electrified fences, machine guns. If we tried to run away, we would either be killed or the Germans would bring us back alive and then kill us. It was a terrible, almost hopeless situation. Every morning at roll call, the Germans would drag the dead bodies of those caught trying to escape the night before to the center of the head-count field as a reminder. A warning. But that didn't stop me from trying to run away. Each one of us thought he could make it — we had to believe in something.

I told the Polish soldier, "Look, I've been walking by the garbage dump and I think I found the shortest and best route out."

The soldier nodded and so right then and there we decided to make our breakout that same night. The rain continued to pour down, a heavy, cold rain. We thought the foul weather would help cover our escape and so planned to make a run immediately after the evening head count. The soldier and his three friends were to come over the fence to my barrack, and then I would lead them out to my route through the cover of the garbage dumps. I warned the soldier that the outer fences were electrified.

He said, "Don't worry about that. We'll take care of them."

At dark, our plan went into effect. One of the soldier's friends didn't show up, so just four of us made our way down the narrow alleyway behind the barracks, through the stinking open latrines and out behind the garbage dump to the electrified fence.

The rain was still heavy, the night as dark as death. But I knew the minute we crossed the outside fence that we would come into a huge open field guarded by soldiers and dogs. We calculated we had thirty seconds to race across the field and lose ourselves in the bordering forest if we were to succeed. I don't remember the distance from the fence to the forest, but it was far. And, remember, the open field held no cover.

Somehow, we crossed that fence safely without being detected.

Then we ran like hell.

Fear makes you run, you know, absolute fear. Even through four months of semi-starvation, your legs somehow find the power to move you when you think you couldn't lift another shovelful of dirt. We made it to the forest but didn't stop there. We kept on running, for hours, barreling through the trees, directionless, dashing madly ahead without thought of where our flight might take us.

Eventually we came to a river. The freezing winter night numbed our bodies and the water surged icy and cold. No one knew how deep it ran; no one had time to stop and think. We plunged in. A strong current pulled me under but I fought it with all the strength I had. Two of the accompanying Polish soldiers were not so lucky. They drowned in the icy water and were swept away before I had a chance to reach them.

Only my Polish soldier friend and I made it to the other side. We stopped to rest against the bank of the river, panting and exhausted. As we rested, the Polish soldier and I discussed where we would go from there. He wanted to go home to the city of Radom. First he had to find different clothing because he was still wearing his Polish uniform. He also knew the Germans would be looking for us. He told me if I heard any noise to climb the highest tree and hide in the branches so the dogs couldn't catch my scent.

The Polish soldier was strong and athletic, and knew what he was talking about. I had seen two people being ripped apart by dogs in the camp and knew the dogs were more dangerous than the SS. But I had also learned how to kill them. If a German Shepherd jumps on you, you stick your hand in his mouth and smack him up in the air. He can only bite your hand a little, but once his feet leave the ground, he becomes powerless. Then one good blow will kill him immediately.

Just as we were talking about how we had to climb a tree, we heard soldiers and dogs barking from our side of the river. Apparently, we had run in a wide circle back to the edge of the camp, not away from it. The Polish solider immediately hoisted himself up a tree. By the time I found my legs and a tree high enough to climb, a huge, snarling German shepherd lunged forward out of the darkness, attacking me from the front. I don't know why — perhaps it was more luck than anything else; certainly it was not because I used my brain — but I struck the dog so hard that I killed him on the spot. I didn't even have time to think about putting my hand in his mouth and throwing him up in the air. When you fear something, you find incredible strength. That I had killed him surprised me, but it didn't stop me from scrambling to the top of the tree, where I sat through the night until the next day.

In the early morning light, three German soldiers came to the clearing and found the dead dog at the bottom of the tree. It never occurred to them to look up, and they went away. Stupid bastards! The Polish soldier and I stayed in the trees for the rest of the day.

And so we survived our first day of freedom.

That evening, when the rain eased a little, we came down. I followed the soldier to a small village to look for something to eat. We found an isolated house at the edge of the forest. The Pole was a specialist at arranging things. He banged on the door and a worried-looking farmer came out holding an axe in his hand. The Polish soldier grabbed the farmer and hit him.

"If you open your mouth," he said, "I'll kill you right here on this spot."

The Pole took the farmer and shut him inside a pig shed, snapping an iron bolt across the wooden door. Inside the farmhouse, he found the farmer's wife and locked her in the bedroom. We looked for different clothes. The soldier found some that fit him, but there were no clothes my size so I wrapped myself in a warm, oversized jacket and then we made our search for food.

Bread.

I tore open the kitchen cupboard, and when I found a beautiful loaf of fresh bread, I thought I had found heaven. I showed the loaf to the soldier, who stared at me as if I were mad and dragged me to the pantry, flung open the cold storage room and pushed me into the hanging sides of beef, sausage, and smoked meat, and the vats of milk.

The soldier knew exactly what to do — he was a great organizer. I only thought of eating right away, of filling the starving hole in my belly. He was smarter. He knew we should grab a sack and fill it with certain kinds of food that would last the longest and get on our way.

In the pantry I found a smoked pig, bacon, sausage, and more loaves of bread, and threw them into a white canvas sack that had once held firewood. Ready to go, I headed for the door.

The soldier stood back and looked at me.

"What's this? You want to go now?" he laughed. "First, we are going to sit down at the table and eat a proper meal. Then we'll leave."

He found a big pot of fresh milk and lifted it to the table.

I thought to myself that if I drank milk now, I would get sick, even though I was desperate to drink.

Instead, I ate loaf after loaf of bread, swallowing half a loaf at a time. But the soldier drank the creamy milk straight from the lip of the jug and, within seconds, doubled over with a bellyache that nearly killed him. I thought he was going to die. I watched him while he writhed on the floor, but I continued to feast. He soon recovered and rejoined me at the table.

Later that night, the soldier and I succeeded in walking ten kilometers[10] more, carrying the sack crammed with salt, matches, and food. We came to another forest and buried ourselves deep in a crevice between two rocks, where we lit a fire. The soldier disappeared and came back shortly afterward with a rooster. I didn't ask where he found it, but I looked at the bird's thick, feathered body with hungry eyes, prepared to eat the bird alive.

But the soldier was not a simple man. He knew the art of survival and practiced it with a finesse I came to appreciate. To cook the rooster, he took dirt from the ground, mixed it with water, then covered the feathers with mud and rolled the bird into the fire. When the smell of the roasted bird wafted into the air, and I looked at this burnt muddy rooster, my heart sank. I had no idea how to eat it.

The soldier waved his hand at me. "Don't worry; it will taste delicious." And he cracked opened the baked shell.

The inside was brown and cooked perfectly. I couldn't tell you if it would taste as delicious today, but, at the time, I was so hungry, so starved, that it was the tastiest bird I had ever eaten. We ate all of it — the bones, the heart, the gizzards. And even after my stomach was bursting, I still felt starved.

During this period of freedom we regained our strength. We stole food from farmhouses, trapped animals, lived off the land. Once we came upon an area swarming with German soldiers. It took quite a few days until we were able to extricate ourselves from the region without getting caught. We had to retreat the way we came. But then, we weren't in a hurry. As long as you are free and not hungry, there is no reason to hurry. Of course, my thoughts during those months continually ran to home. I wanted to get home. I didn't consider that my family would not be there. The belief that they were still alive, still waiting for me, sitting at the kitchen table, my mother's hands twisting her white handkerchief with worry, pulled me back home. Home. It sounded so safe.

We had now come to a new part of Poland that I recognized as only two hundred kilometers[11] from our farm. At this juncture, the soldier advised me to continue along with him to his home town. He promised to help me find work. I don't think he knew I was Jewish. We never discussed it. I don't even know if being Jewish would have mattered to him. He was a good man. But I told him I had to go home.

Before we separated, we scrounged enough food for the both of us. That night we said goodbye to each other and parted. I don't know what would have happened to me if I had gone along with him.

I don't know what happened to him. I never saw him again.

After he left, I felt completely lost. I didn't know whether to go here or there. It took a long while for me to get used to being alone. It's always harder when you're alone. Do you know that in our two months together, I never learned much about the soldier, not even his name. We never spoke about personal things. In survival, you watch out for yourself, you close yourself up.

So, I continued on by myself, wandering about the forest. I think I must have been only a day's walk from home, but I never got there. The Polish police caught me in a tiny village where I had been stupid enough to wander about in the fields in daylight.

First they beat me; then they dragged me to the police station and interrogated me, asking me over and over again who I was, where did I come from? I didn't tell them anything and they beat me again. So I lied and said I was an orphan. They didn't care and they didn't believe me.

They continued to beat me until I was black and blue, my face broken, my arms twisted. If they had any brains, they would have pulled down my pants and seen at once I was a Jew, but even for this they were too stupid. They just knew how to beat, not to think.

In the end, they sent me back to Pustkow, the same labor camp I had escaped from only two months before. My despair was complete — a mixture of pain from my wounds and pain from my own stupidity at being caught.

And so ended my first escape.

CHAPTER FOUR: The Breakout

At Pustkow things had changed. The camp had turned from a labor camp into a concentration camp. Things were a bit more organized — prisoners who were strong, worked. Those who became sick or weak, died — an efficient system. And for those who had escaped and had been found, our fate was sealed with a death certificate. My expectations were not high.

At the camp an unwritten code existed: Prisoners do not inform on each other. If one of us happened to break this code, his neck would also get broken. It was that simple and that effective.

When I was returned to Pustkow, my former fellow inmates acted as though they had never seen me before, even though the guards kept insisting I had been a prisoner there. I denied it, of course, and they couldn't prove it. The Germans had not yet developed the tattooed-arm numbering system for quick identification. The number, you see, came later, at another camp.

They assigned me to another barrack and I went to work carrying lumber from underneath a bridge that spanned a river. I was continually watched by a tall, blond, German soldier with an SS insignia of high rank and knee-high leather boots who flicked his whip in my direction whenever my pace slackened. He recognized me and I recognized him. He watched me for a while, but I feigned ignorance. Then he called over to a kapo who also knew me from my first imprisonment.

"Do you know this one?" he demanded. "Wasn't he the one

who escaped a few months ago?"

The kapo trembled with fear. Although he worked for the Germans, he was actually a prisoner himself. He knew that if he told on me, he would be condemned to certain death by the other inmates. His dilemma was complete. The SS commander cracked his whip and demanded the kapo confess and tell him the truth. He was certain I was an escapee. But the kapo would not speak.

Furious, the SS commander screamed at the kapo in German and shackled him to a wooden post. He raised his whip and slashed his face until the kapo collapsed and finally said, "Yes, this is the one!"

By now, however, the SS commander didn't believe the kapo. Yet he still wasn't convinced. He grabbed me, tied me against a railing, roped my hands behind my back, stood back and lashed me with the whip. He slashed at my back, my buttocks, my legs, my face, again and again, ripping my skin into shreds, searing me with a pain I shall never forget and an animosity I will never let go of. If I should ever meet that animal, that barbarian again, I would rip him apart with my bare hands, you can believe me. He whipped me with a ferocity equaled only by the attack of the dogs.

I remember counting to ten; then I fell into unconsciousness, which angered the SS commander even more. He threw cold water on my face to revive me and whipped me again, tearing the skin from my back and face, ripping off the skin from my buttocks. When he finished, he left me tied to the post for three days.

It took almost half a year to recover from those wounds. I'll tell you something: I shall never forget that animal's face until I die. If I had a whip and I saw him now, I would slash him to pieces.

I could not go back to the fields for a month. To stay alive, I worked inside the camp collecting garbage. Some of my wounds healed right away. Others never did. They became infected or would heal and then when I sat down or made a jerking movement, they would break open again.

Luckily, by the end of the month, the Germans transferred me and one hundred other prisoners to East Prussia, Germany, near Danzig (Gdansk) on the Baltic Sea, where we found ourselves working in a submarine factory built within the work camp.

It was 1940 and I was now a man of thirteen and a half years. I went to work in the factory as a welder. The camp conditions were an improvement over Pustkow. The East Prussian camp was cleaner. At least they had showers, although the food was worthless. Breakfast consisted of a half-liter of tea at four o'clock in the morning; dinner at nine at night equaled 120 grams of bread and soup. I worked at the submarine factory for about one year. I had a chance to heal from my whip wounds because an inmate who happened to be a doctor sewed up the festering sores on my buttocks with electrical wire he had stolen from work. Those slashes hurt me for a long time. Even today I still feel them pinch me when I sit.

This camp was not what you know of today as a concentration camp. Most of the prisoners were gentiles — Poles rounded up to work for the Germans. They had no idea I was a Jew. We were housed in a barrack of one thousand people. Twelve of us were given one bunk to share. There were no beds, just tiered wooden slats, one on top of another, and we lay across them horizontally, our feet hanging over the sides, to make more room. Human shelving. The camp was a labor camp, yes, but don't think for a moment they didn't still hang people, shoot people, beat people. They just hadn't advanced yet to the mass ovens.

It was at the submarine work camp that I received my first tattoo — a small number, almost invisible. Because twelve people had to share one tiered wooden bunk "bed," we got to know each other very well. In my bunk were two Silesians and a few Poles. After a long while, when we grew to trust each other, we began to talk about escaping. But you couldn't plan an escape for just a few people when there were twelve people listening in the same bed. So, during the night, our group would huddle and talk about a major breakout.

In our group was a forty-year-old Silesian. He had been in prison probably half his life and was a crackerjack criminal, a technical expert of the first class. He could crack safes, blow fuses, short the electricity with great speed. Because of his experience, he was the major planner of the breakout. A short, stocky, athletic boxer of a man, whom we simply called "*Pan*" (Polish for "Boss"). He had a cadre of friends who were plumbers, electricians, thieves. Among them, they planned the escape down to the last minute detail.

We worked on the breakout for three months until everything was ready: wire-clippers acquired, wrenches, knives, matches, wire, and tape slowly but cleanly lifted from the stockrooms or worktables of the submarine factory.

One day, the Boss came by a hell of a beating. I don't know why. The Germans didn't need reasons. When he came back to the barrack, or rather, when they dragged him back, the Boss was black and blue from head to foot and could barely move. I have never seen anyone beaten so savagely, so cruelly. It took the Boss a week to come around. I think he probably survived solely because he was in good physical shape; he had a sportsman's physique.

When the Boss was able to move his lips, he whispered, "The minute I am able to run, I won't wait a minute longer."

During the next few days as he healed, the Boss organized the final tools for our escape: shears to cut wires, wrenches, pliers to short the electricity, everything we needed to break through the electrified fences.

And then the moment came when he was ready and we would wait no longer.

We had two major considerations, one being that we were dressed in striped uniforms that could be seen a kilometer away, and two, that all twelve of us had to run away together, even if one didn't want to, because if that one person chose to stay behind, the Germans wouldn't leave him alive.

At dinner, the Boss gave us all an extra bit of bread. Where he came by it, I don't know. He was the Boss and we did what we were told. He instructed us carefully on the arrangements: how we were to bury our clothes after we found replacements, how we had to run and in which direction.

It was a beautiful summer night. Clear, light. We had absolutely no protection from the weather. But he was adamant about escaping then. There was no turning back.

To get out, we had to cross two fences. The first was not a problem. It was not electrified. The Boss swiftly cut the thin wires and we crawled through to the other side. The second fence was charged with electricity and wound its way around the camp. Directly behind the fence were guards in watchtowers, one tower every fifty meters. The guards stood armed with machine guns and searchlights.

"We are not going through the fence in the middle of the field," the Boss whispered to us as we slid across the ground from the first to the second fence. "We are going to cut through right under their noses."

He was smart, that Boss, because if we cut through the next fence as close as possible to the watch tower, the guards would have trouble seeing us, unless they looked straight down toward the base of the tower. Because the second fence was electrified, the moment a wire was cut a bell would ring in the watchtower and lights would flash an alarm.

As we neared the second fence, the Boss instructed each of us to cut a different wire. He gave the signal. Our shears hit the wires at the same moment and twelve lights and twelve bells rang out all over the camp like a pinball machine.

All hell broke loose.

Shots rang out from all directions.

We scrambled through the fence. Only seven of us made it. Three were hit. One of the inmates fell seriously wounded. He screamed out the Boss's name. His voice rang through the night, which was already sounding off with bullets, alarms, dogs barking and machine-gun fire. We could see the fellow entangled in the barbed wire, blood gushing from his throat.

The Boss, who was already tearing through the fields, stopped in his tracks and raced back to the fence. He killed his friend with one swift, merciful blow and broke into a mad run.

We bolted through the fields, running for hours, stopping only when the sun rose. Fear creates strength and so our weak legs held us up in flight. Do you know what it is to run without stopping from eleven in the night until sunrise?

By the second night we found a lone farmhouse in the foothills of the mountains. The Boss entered the cottage and put everything in order. I didn't see what he did, just the results: a robust farm girl kicking on the bed in the back room, pantry doors swept wide open, food piled high across the wooden table.

The rest of us waited outside until the Boss had completed his work. One of the men found a pig in the yard and went to catch it. The pig squealed as if someone had just put an axe to its throat. The hog's screams echoed through the farm like a murderous alarm. The Boss rushed out of the house.

"Leave that pig alone, idiot," he ordered. "You'll wake up the whole damn village!"

The pig slid through the man's startled hands and waddled with smug satisfaction to a corner of the sty and stuffed his nose into the dirt. The Boss rubbed his hands on his sides, brushed his way past us, grabbed another pig, and without blinking, hacked off his head with a carving knife and threw the pig into his sack, his hind quarters still squirming. We would enjoy that pig for several days.

The Boss disappeared back inside the house. I followed him, finding the pantry filled with cheeses, butter, bread and big vats of sour milk. I didn't care if I would double over in pain; I drank the sour milk down to the very bottom of the pot and then, still starving, stuffed my mouth with anything I could find.

And so began my second escape and another short-lived period of freedom.

CHAPTER FIVE: The Tarnow Ghetto

The seven of us continued along through the forests toward Poland. We walked for the next four months, during the night, careful to avoid being caught, keeping away from the main roads and people, even if we had to walk twenty kilometers[12] out of the way to keep to the forest. We also found our food at night: fat chickens from backyard coops, pigs, birds.

I knew now there were no Jews left in the big towns. We had heard this news from the prisoners who had come through the camps from East Prussia. They talked about "ghettos". I didn't know what a ghetto was. I had never heard the word before. One of the Jewish prisoners explained that the Germans had concentrated all the Jews into one selected section of each city. So in a vague sort of way I understood that my parents would not be at the farm, but I thought perhaps that they would be in the ghetto of the district's central city, Tarnow.[13] I decided to head straight for there.

Four months later I came to the outskirts of Tarnow.

By this time, most of our group had split up, leaving only the Boss and me together. He was in no hurry to get anywhere. If he went home, I suppose he would have been caught again and sent back to prison. So instead, he led me to Tarnow and there we parted.

We stopped by a small village outside the city walls where we hid in the woods for a day and a night. I felt tremendously sad about leaving the Boss. We talked about meeting again. He knew where I came from and took down all the particulars on a piece of paper, but he didn't tell me anything more about himself. I only knew he came from an area that was nearer to the German border. He wouldn't have told me more, because I am sure he was quite a well-established criminal. I'm glad for that, let me tell you, because he taught me how to survive. And if a criminal like that should have such a good heart, such sharp wits, then I don't consider being a criminal such a despicable profession.

The Boss was a wizard at languages. He spoke German perfectly, as well as Polish and French. He said he was a professional electrician. My guess? A professional thief. Why? Because he had been imprisoned for a good many years before I met up with him. When the Boss was in a good mood, he would tell us about his adventures in different prisons — what they did there, how they ate, how they made trouble for the guards...you know. He was in tip-top shape, that Boss, his body a shell-casing of steel. He looked like a boxer: short, squat, muscled, and he had greater physical and mental power than the seven of us combined. He would always carry the heaviest sack of food. He was the strongest, the toughest. I respected him. I learned so much from him. He was the Boss. We listened to his every word. Ah, how I would love to see that man again.

That last night, the day before we separated, we stood on the roof of a burned-out house and waited to see what was going on inside the brick walls of the city of Tarnow. From the roof we could see hundreds of people marching in and out of an opening in the walls bordered by barricades and police guards. The ghetto. A fortress. It looked impossible to just walk in there.

The Boss was clever. He instructed me how to get inside the walls. Together from the cottage roof, we watched the movement in and out of the ghetto. In the morning, groups of bedraggled men and women marched outside to work in the fields. At five o'clock, they returned. The Boss, having studied the work formation carefully, pulled me to him and said, "Look, you have only one possibility of getting inside the ghetto. During the time that the biggest group of people march back inside the walls, jump into their lines and that's that."

There was one problem. Clothing. I had found wonderfully warm clothing months back; a thick fleece-lined winter jacket, woolen trousers, a heavy shirt, socks, and solid leather boots. But the people coming in and out of the ghetto were wearing rags, threadbare clothing. I was so determined to get inside that I discarded my warm clothing, tore at my shirt, smeared my face with the ashes from the burnt cinders of the house and prepared to join them.

Before the Boss and I parted at the unhinged gate of the farmhouse, the Boss looked at me and said, "I hope you find what you're looking for. And if you survive, and if I survive, we shall see each other again."

I was too young and too hardened by then to read the meaning in his words and expression. To find my family was all that concerned me. If I knew then what I was soon to learn, I would never have left him.

And then I was alone.

The Boss disappeared into the forest as if he had never existed. This was the second time I had been left by myself. It's a miserable, isolating feeling. But my determination to find my family overrode my desire to stay with him.

How I suffered that night. I clutched onto the roof and sank against the smoldering ruins, feeling as if I had just given away the last thread of life. The day broke cloudy and rainy. I took refuge inside what was left of the house and waited for the evening, when I finally saw a large contingent of people, perhaps six hundred or so, return from their day of work. There weren't many guards, just a few Polish policemen who looked as though they were cold and wanted to get the workers back into the ghetto so they could go home.

I walked down to the road, brushing alongside the body of people and as the group passed in formation, I quickly jumped between their rows. And that is how I got inside the Tarnow Ghetto.

The Germans and Poles had restricted the living quarters of the Jews to a few streets and built high walls of brick around the area. There was only one entrance and exit into and out of the ghetto. Later, someone told me that the first ghetto in Poland was built in Tarnow. The bastards! My district's main city had the distinction of being the first in their destruction of the Polish Jews and my family. It all began and ended there.

From the moment I marched through the gates into the gray streets filled with ragged Jews, hungry children, rats, broken or boarded windows, I felt the cold run through my torn shirt. The sights within the walls left me more depressed than I believed possible.

I immediately hustled through the streets, tapping on this one's shoulder, knocking on that door to ask if anyone knew or had seen my brothers or my parents. And do you know, can you believe that in this four-block area of 150,000 Jews, not one soul would speak with me! No one would answer my questions. They looked through me as if I didn't exist. Most scurried away in fear like rats.

In the morning when they sent the Jews off to work, I hid in basements and stared through the grilled windows at every face that passed by in the streets, but I did not recognize a soul.

You cannot imagine the despair and hopelessness I felt. I sat hungry, cold, and so very much alone. No one wanted to let a stranger into his house. No one would talk to me. This sank me lower in spirit than any of the time I had spent in the camps. I even began to think the camps were better than this utter and complete isolation. By the fifth day I was completely broken. I didn't know what to do anymore. Here I had made such extreme efforts to get to Tarnow, to get into Tarnow, to get into this ghetto, this prison of Jews without faces, without hearts, and for what? I should have gone on with the Boss.

It was late Friday evening. I knew it must be Friday because I saw the Sabbath candles burning in the window of one lone, lovely house that stood at the end of a quiet street. The last street in the ghetto.

When I passed by the window, I smelled bread baking and food cooking. My stomach twisted in pain. I knew at once this was a home of wealthy Jews. I was so hungry, I decided to bang on the door and ask for some food. I didn't care what they would say. I wanted food.

I climbed up the brick stairs, pushed on the front entrance door and entered a wide foyer with stairs that separated the first floor from the second. I turned and stared at the heavy oak door to the first-floor apartment and, with determination, lifted my hand to the brass door knocker and then banged the handle against the wood. I waited a long time and banged again until someone finally came and opened the door.

A thin, elderly man looked down at me through a monocle, his face flooded with fear.

"Who are you?" he asked. His voice rose and grew ugly. "What do you want? Go away from here!"

I explained I was looking for my family, with such and such a name, from the town of Gromnik.

"I don't know anybody like that," he answered. His voice dropped to a whisper. He looked nervously around beyond the door to the street and said, "Go away from here!"

I was so angry, so furious with him, I slammed the door with such force that it hit the man square in the face, dropping his spectacle to the ground with a crunch. I didn't care what happened to him. The hour was late. I had become numb with cold and was starving, depressed, and more alone than I had ever felt. I hated him. I hated their warm, cozy house with a table filled with bread and meats. I hated those Jews, all of them.

The hell with them! I would be damned if I went out into the cold again. I stormed up the stairs to the second floor and then continued up to the roof to look for a place to sleep. By now I decided I had had enough of the ghetto. In the morning I would find a way to escape.

In the meantime I burrowed behind the staircase under the roof. The cold winter air blew through a hole in the rafters and bit at my body. I cursed having thrown away my warm clothes. I hadn't eaten in over three days and felt more exhausted than I had in all the months working in the submarine factory. Complete and total despair.

For the first time in the thirteen years of my life, I came to think that life just wasn't worth living. To live with such despair, such hopelessness, without family, a home, without friends, to live by wits and cunning just to stay alive — what was the purpose of it all? I came very close that night to letting myself let go of life.

In the middle of the night, I jerked awake to a barrage of machine-gun fire from the streets below. I heard volley after volley of continuous shooting, people yelling, babies howling, children screaming, the streets ablaze with torches, machine-gun fire ripping through the windows, bayonets pounding at the doors.

"*Achtung! Juden heraus!*" (Jews out of the house!) soldiers were shouting.

Hundreds of Germans stormed every building. "To the street! Everyone out and into the street!"

I peeped out of the hole in the roof and saw hundreds, perhaps even thousands of Jews rounded up, dragged out of their houses into the streets, pushed into open-backed trucks. Babies ripped from mothers' arms, bayoneted, shot, thrown in the alleys, women separated from men, old men beaten with clubs, young men lined up and shot against the walls.

I quickly thought about what I should do — go down to the

street or hide where I was? I peeked down the staircase. I saw the stuffy old Jews from this rich house run down the basement stairs to their bunkers. Many families had bunkers in those days, but they couldn't hide from the Germans.

The soldiers smashed the front door open and swarmed into the hallway catching the whole family before they made it down the stairs, and dragged them away.

I watched as if I had no soul. I didn't give a damn about those people. I felt no fear, no feelings. I had turned off the switch a long time ago — somewhere back in that first camp. I watched the holocaust of that night like another in a series of a world gone mad that no longer held meaning for me.

They took that family away, the Germans, and they never came back.

The Germans never found me. I lay still under the snow and hay, tucked behind the stairs to the roof. And I waited.

Finally, by early morning, the streets became quiet again. Deathly quiet. Not a soul moved outside, nor were there sounds from the houses along the street. They stood in silent witness — doors wide open, empty of people — to the night of horror that had swept their floors clean of all inhabitants.

And there were no soldiers.

I crawled out of my hole and crept downstairs. I searched the rooms cautiously for soldiers, people...but met only silence. Feeling relatively safe, I went to the first floor and entered the apartment that had been closed to me only the night before. The heavy wooden door stood wide open, hanging askew on its hinges. The whole apartment had been turned up on its legs; tables, chairs, cabinets smashed, lights dangling, closets ripped open, clothes scattered on the floor, suitcases dumped in haste. I'll never forget the sight. Still, I felt nothing.

More to the point, I threw off my filthy shirt and work pants, dug through the closets and wriggled into the best and warmest clothing I could find. I took a good pair of shoes, a warm leather jacket with fur lining, and a flannel shirt and heavy woolen trousers.

And then I sat down to eat.

I don't know how long I stayed there eating — maybe four or five days. Anyway, it didn't matter. No one came in. The soldiers had long gone from the ghetto. There were no Jews left for them. I took my time. I never went out. I ate more than I had ever eaten before. It was like a continual feast; whatever door, whatever cabinet I opened, behind the walls, under the shelves, in the closets, I would find more food — tins of paté, smoked meats, cheeses, fish, everything, anything. Whatever I found, I ate right there on the spot. But believe me, I never felt full.

After those few days, I thought about my next move. Again I began to look for a way out of that godforsaken ghetto. At night I crept across the rooftops, searching house to house, looking for an escape, but I couldn't ever seem to find a way over the wall where the SS wouldn't be waiting for me. The situation seemed hopeless.

One night, from the roof, I saw an open sewer. Not too far beyond the manhole was a Polish street. I decided to try to make it to the Polish side right away. I slid down the manhole into the sewer and crawled on all fours through the dirt, slime, urine and feces for a few hundred meters until I came to a screen cover. I looked through the screen and saw that I had made it to the Polish street. I crept forward. The pipes began to narrow and I searched frantically for an exit. A short distance farther down the sewer, I saw another manhole cover and pushed my weight against it, but it wouldn't budge. I shoved against the steel, strained and pushed, but it just wouldn't move. As I crawled on, the sewer narrowed and I couldn't pass any further.

It was freezing down in that sewer. I was soaking wet and stinking with human waste. I stopped. I had lost my sense of direction in the dark and even if I had tried to go back, I wasn't sure I'd find the same route. A sewer has many different channels, a maze of refuse and excrement.

In the blackness, I retreated. Somehow, I found myself underneath that same stubborn manhole cover. This time, when I tried to lift it, the cover eased open without any trouble. I poked my head through the hole and saw a horse and carriage drive off. The horse had been standing on the manhole.

Luck, however, wasn't with me. From all my travels through the sewers, I came out only one hundred meters[14] from the exit of the ghetto — one hundred slimy, stinking, waste-filled meters. Just as I raised the sewer cover, two soldiers passed by...and collared me.

And that was the end of that.

CHAPTER SIX: Mielec

The soldiers returned me to the ghetto like a whipped dog. They took me to a building where hundreds of men were being held before being sent off to the camps. My clothes and body stank. Luckily, in the big room there were showers and toilets. At least it was organized. I give the Germans some credit. Probably because of my overwhelming stench and their best interests, the other prisoners managed to locate a shirt, a pair of trousers and underwear for me to change into.

The Jews inside came from all over Poland. The Germans defeated us before we knew what was happening by separating families from the same town, inhabitants of the same region and people of the same nationality. I suppose that's the reason I never found anyone from my own family or anyone I knew in Tarnow.

The next morning they threw us into trucks and drove us to Mielec, a camp in the west of Poland. This time I didn't care. I had lost the strength and will to have another go-around. Yet, I survived. Don't ask me why. I didn't think at the time I really wanted to.

At Mielec, they tattooed me with the letters you see on my wrist: KL, *Konzentration Lager* (Concentration Camp).[15] I wear it forever. It is something you can never hide. Never. Look at our friend, Shoshanah, how she gouged out the blue ink from her arm, how even the best plastic surgeon in Israel couldn't smooth over those marks. It is with her like it is with me, forever and ever; when I shower, when I wake up in the morning, when I sleep, when I roll up my sleeve, when I wash. Shoshanah has a scar, and I have blue ink on my arm. What difference does it make? In the end, we were the children of a hideous twist of events that you couldn't possibly understand. Yet, here we sit, and I recite to you all I can remember and I sound like a robot, without feelings, mechanically telling you about beatings, killings, living from minute to minute like a dog. Worse, like a Jew.

And I wonder why I can no longer feel. Perhaps tonight I shall sleep badly, the dreams will come. They do when I think back to those years, and yet I am telling you all of this. I don't know why. I never told Amit or Avi or Shimone, my own sons. They never asked and you ask. Why do you want to know about this? And why do I tell you?

I think sometimes I'm not quite normal. I don't feel like others do. I don't know how to cry, to feel sad, to mourn when a friend dies. Something is wrong with me, I know that. And I envy people who do feel, do love, do cry. I wish I knew how to cry. Perhaps it would help.

You know, when they drove those trucks back inside the gates of the camp I felt a sense of relief that I belonged somewhere, no longer lost in the wilderness. They were clever, those Germans. I hated them and I respected them. It must sound like an odd match: hate, fear, and a respect for their efficient, systematic destruction of your very sense of self. Like scientists, they manipulated us. They knew exactly how to do it. I was home. Can you understand that? The camps were all I knew. Now you want to know and I'll tell you how it was:

Before we found our bunks, they sent us directly to the showers for delousing, which meant passing through a series of sprays from a long line of nozzles. As we exited, we were handed Polish army clothes with a yellow patch on our backs and over one knee so we couldn't run too far without being marked. They sheared our hair down the middle of our heads and left the sides long so the stripe would always indicate we were prisoners if we should ever run away.[16]

That winter I went barefoot. They took my shoes. I found pieces of board and tied them to my feet with rags. Survival. Somehow you learned to exist on nothing.

I must explain to you just how everything looked so you can try to see it, smell it: Imagine the barracks lined with three-tiered bunks, layer after layer, bunk against bunk like a stack of wooden cards, gouged wood, rough planks that served as beds for twelve men to lie horizontally on each tier. No mattresses, no blankets, wearing the same clothing they handed you on the first day, lying atop planks of raw wood next to warm bodies that more often than not would grow cold and stiff in death during the night.

Toilets did not exist. Instead we dug deep trenches behind the barracks that quickly came to stink like a backed-up cesspool. Dysentery ran rampant through our camp, killing off most of the population. But as quickly as one man would die, a new truckload of prisoners would be brought in to replace him. Remember, I was thirteen going on fourteen. A man-child. And I only knew one thing — that to survive, I must work. I worked for five years, each day twenty-four hours of grotesque brutality. A day was twenty-four hours long if you died. If you survived, it felt like a year. I became an old man at age fourteen.

On this same first day, I already knew the system quite well. I knew what would happen but I spoke to no one. I didn't tell anyone I had been in a camp before. I just kept my mouth shut and waited.

The next morning during roll call, the soldiers asked us what our professions were and I found myself lying with relative ease about being a steel cutter. I had heard they needed operators to work in the Henklewerks airplane factory, a Polish plant taken over by the Germans for their war effort. I learned my profession at the Henklewerks factory — how to use a lathe, cut steel, fabricate metal, fix engine parts. It is all I know to this day. Look at my fingers. I try to clean the grease from my nails every night after work, but I am still just a simple mechanic. My brother Paul is a tailor. We both learned our professions from the Germans — Paul, cutting out coarse, prison-striped concentration camp coverings and me, cutting steel for the German fighter planes, the Messerschmidts.

But I am straying from the story. I want you to know that

Mielec was a hard camp. We were given barely any food. Many, many people got sick and died of dysentery. We prisoners worked two shifts, each twelve hours long, plus three hours standing in the field for head counts, seven days a week. On Sundays, if you managed to survive the week, you were given one half-day's rest.

It is hard to explain the physical setup. Henklewerks was quite a well-known factory and stood within the grounds of our camp. Most of the inmates worked at the plant. Its size was mammoth.

Surprisingly, although perhaps not so because I was a good worker, I grew to have good relations with the German work managers. They sent me to study at a special technical class on airplane construction they held twice a week within the camp. Imagine me, Yonah Steiner, age fourteen, studying airplane engineering with fifteen German soldiers and SS officers. The thought made my skin crawl.

The work manager, Herr Euwecker, informed me that I had to take this course. He didn't ask me if I wanted to go. He sent me. Of course I didn't want to go. It could only make my life more of a hell, add more hours to my work day. And I felt inadequate. Strange to admit it now, why I felt so inadequate, but I didn't know German that well. I was afraid I wouldn't understand the lectures. I also didn't want to be forced to learn anything that would help the Germans win the war.

It went this way: Each one of us had been given a card with a seat number typed on it. To my surprise and no small horror, I found myself sitting between two SS officers.

Herr Euwecker was a good man, even though he was a Nazi. When I returned to the factory from the class, he asked me, "So, what did you think?" His lieutenant stood next to him. The lieutenant was also a good man. He liked me. He wasn't like the others. But as I said, I was a good worker. So I told them both exactly how I felt.

"Tell me," I said, "How did such a *haftlink* like me get a place inbetween such high ranking officers of the SS? It makes me uncomfortable. Can you please arrange it so I can be moved to the other side of the room?"

The lieutenant turned and discussed my request with Euwecker, who immediately picked up the telephone. "You will not change your seat," he said after he hung up the phone. "But the SS will treat you with respect. I give you my promise they will not bother you."

And at the next lesson, the two SS officers had changed their attitude. One brought me a sandwich. 1 sat down, stunned by their deference. Sometimes when the instructor asked technical questions, one of my SS neighbors would turn and nudge my arm.

"Why don't you answer?" he would ask. "I know you know the right answer."

Then I would have to explain that my German wasn't fluent enough.

"Tell me, then," he would say, "and I'll answer for you."

I often told him and helped that SS officer during his exams to become a pilot. I did it for sandwiches, bread, slices of meat. I sold all the knowledge I had. And then slowly I began to relax and enjoy this small amount of "pull" I had acquired. They came to treat me well, those soldiers. To survive, one does what one has to do.

Not long afterwards, the same pilot trainee brought a group of soldiers to my section of the factory and asked me to explain the work I did. I kept my mouth shut. Imagine the looks on the other prisoners' faces down the huge assembly line as I am being encircled by a group of Nazis officers. They were certain I was going to die. I agreed with them.

Herr Euwecker, fat, stuffy Euwecker, came running out of his office and nervously plucked at the collar of his shirt, kicked me back into life and told me to explain what I did.

I explained. In the camps, you see, you learn through bitter experience not to speak without permission. With permission, I spoke freely. Euwecker was pleased.

After the Nazis departed, I was rewarded with two kilograms[17] of bread and one hundred cigarettes instead of the hanging that I was sure would follow. I became a rich man. On our black market system, a loaf of bread was equivalent to twenty American dollars. Five cigarettes could buy you one piece of bread, 120 grams. The same moment Euwecker handed me the bread, three other fellow prisoners were standing beside me. I cut the bread into thirds and we stuffed the slices into our mouths. In the camps you learned never to save anything because someone would just as quickly steal it.

At the same time, I spent extra hours in the night making cigarette lighters from scraps of chrome metal. 1 would sell them to the Germans. One lighter bought one piece of bread. I would sneak back into the factory and work at night. There were fewer guards then. The SS thought I was working on a special project, but all the while I was busy changing the drill heads on the machinery to punch out the different parts of the lighters. Once all the different sections were completed, I assembled them and sold them. Without this moonlighting operation, you simply could not survive.

But my fame at the camp didn't come from lighters. It came from an ashtray I had modeled after one of the Messerschmidts. It was a beautiful piece of work cut from aluminum and steel. A perfect replica.

One night our Jewish guard fell asleep and an SS guard came in and saw me constructing this model. I felt my face pale. My mouth went dry. I knew right then I had reached the end of my life. I was certain he would kill me on the spot. There was no possible way to hide what I was doing. The model lay in a thousand pieces on the table in front of me.

He beat me, that officer, good and hard, smashing my face into the metal table, snapping my nose with his fists, twisting my ears, my head. And when he was satisfied he had left his mark on me, he said, "Put this mess together!"

Through the blood and pain, I managed to assemble the airplane as quickly as possible. The officer took the shiny model in his hand and circled it above his head under the light, examining the sides, the details. It was a beautiful airplane. Not that it was it the first model I had ever made. If he had opened up the machine body and stuck his fist into the oil, he would have found a dozen more.

"This is very nice." He smacked his lips and held the model out of my reach. "Whom are you making it for?"

I told him one of the soldiers ordered me to make it.

The officer raised his eyebrows and said, "We shall see about this. Tomorrow morning I shall make an inquiry."

He took the model.

In the morning he returned with a group of SS officers and went straight to Herr Euwecker. I thought it would certainly be my end now. I watched through the glass doors that divided the factory from the offices and saw the bastard hand Euwecker the model.

"I caught that one making this model in the middle of the night!" he said, and pointed an accusing finger at me through the glass partition.

Euwecker stood up, puffed out his stomach and held his hand out for the ashtray model. One by one, each man inspected my work until it made the complete round of hands. That was all I saw.

When the shifts changed, we stood in our lines to march out. A voice came over the loud speaker and called my number. I knew I was doomed. And everyone else in the line knew it as well.

I walked out of my row and went into the office.

My face was so swollen from the beating, Euwecker barely recognized me. The lieutenant gasped, stood back and asked who had beaten me. I pointed to the SS guard. Then he asked why.

I answered, "I made a present for your office without asking permission."

The lieutenant said nothing. He stood there considering my words. In the meantime, all my fellow workers were still standing on line waiting for me. They couldn't go back to their barracks until I joined them, alive or dead. They were quite irritated and looked at me hoping for a speedy resolution in either direction.

After what seemed like an eternity, the lieutenant finally said to Euwecker, "He hasn't done anything except make a present for the office. He didn't know he had to ask permission."

Euwecker heaved himself up from the table and faced me. "Who did this to you?" he asked as if he had never heard the lieutenant's original question.

Again I pointed to the SS.

Ignoring the guard, Euwecker telephoned for a doctor to come treat my face.

After the SS left, I caught hell.

"It is forbidden to do what you did!" Euwecker stormed. "Not without permission! Where did you get the material to make models? Where did you find the time?"

I explained that I had constructed the models from scrap materials. It wasn't true. I really came by the aluminum from another Jew who also worked extra hours to stay alive. He stole it from the storeroom. One hand washes the other. *Avodot fouche* we called it.

But this wasn't the end of it.

My co-prisoners were still standing on line, waiting, all of them angry because they weren't able to go to sleep or to eat without me, and soon enough they would have to wake up and go back to work. Finally I was allowed to return to the line. Afterwards, one of the SS called me out and took me to the infirmary, where they sewed up my face.

Two weeks later, I was called again to the office.

Herr Euwecker asked, "How long does it take you to build those model ashtrays and airplanes?"

I told him I had never looked at the clock.

He said, "I'll give you a work order to make ten of these models. But although I give you the order, I will not write down the hours you need to do this. So just don't get caught. But if you are caught, show the requisition."

Now I tried to make these models so I would get caught — by the same SS guard.

Our relations did not end smoothly.

It happened on a Sunday after the second shift. The SS guard came in. As he walked closer to me, I pulled out a piece of ashtray and put it on the table.

He came and looked down at the work. "So, you're making it again," he snarled.

I didn't answer him. I walked over to the cabinet and pulled out my work-order card and shoved it under his nose.

"Oh, now it's all right," he nodded. "But I want one, too."

"If you want one," I said, "bring me a work order."

His voice turned angry. He shouted, "It's written on the order: a requisition for ten. Make eleven!"

I told him I wasn't free to do it without a work order.

Everyday he came and asked for his model.

Every day I told him, "With a work order, I'll make you a hundred. I don't care."

When I finished all ten, I brought them to the office and received bread and a package of cakes. What you don't do for bread! But that SS officer never got even one ashtray.

However, he was always lurking around, hoping to catch me.

But he never did. Once he threw a hard piece of metal at me and it cut open the main artery on my wrist. I squeezed my arm and went to the office. They administered first aid, and then took me to the infirmary, where they told me I couldn't work for a week. In the camps, work is survival, so I went right back to the factory.

But this little story is only one small incident in the daily, minute-to-minute histories of survival.

CHAPTER SEVEN: Flossenburg

One biting cold winter day after the work head count, I was ordered along with 200 other men into a cattle car. It seemed they were taking only the professionals away — the experts in welding, munitions, engineering. Apparently I was considered a professional in airplane construction.

The year was 1943. I must have been fifteen years old, but I felt as if I had passed fifty — fifty hard, dangerous years, years that held no sign that the carnage would ever end. During that period, there was not even a flicker of hope. The Germans were murdering, slaughtering each and every one of us in every corner, in every place. There was no hope, I tell you, none, absolutely no hope that things would change.

In Mielec we used to hear from the Germans how the war was progressing. At this time, I thought the Germans would win. There never seemed any other possibility. The Germans were cocky bastards. All they did was laugh at the Americans and English, so sure were they of defeating them. We could tell when the war was going well for the Germans: we would get an extra piece of bread. When things were bad, we were beaten or killed. Every one of the prisoners hoped the Americans and English would win, but there seemed no chance it could happen.

On that winter day, we were herded into the railway cars. They didn't tell us where we were going. Or why. We traveled for many days, receiving food only when we stopped at certain stations along the route. The German guards would pull open the freight doors. We would throw out the dead and they would throw in some scraps of food and a full bucket of water.

In our car there had been twenty men. Ten died along the way. And it seemed the trip would never end. There was barely room to lie down. The car stank of urine and human waste. For toilets they gave us one pail, or we used a hole in the floorboards. That might have been sufficient, but the shaking of the train jerked the pail over, forcing us to live like animals in our own waste. When we stopped at a station, which occurred infrequently, the guards would let us out and we would squat by the side of the train. Sometimes soldiers tossed in fresh hay, but the stench of the dead and the stink of the urine and feces rode with us.

As I told you before, one gets used to seeing dead people. It ceased to affect me. I got used to it. We all got used to it. Because we weren't alive ourselves. We could be just as dead in another hour or two. You just never knew. We traveled side by side with the dead until we reached a station. Sometimes it could be as long as five days. Do you know I used to think there was more life in a piece of wood than in the bodies that were piled next to me?

Finally we reached our destination: Flossenburg. Once again I was back in Germany.

The train ran directly into the camp. We arrived at night and the SS kept us inside the cattle cars until morning. Those of us who had any strength left in our legs stood and looked out a small window in our car. The camp looked huge. I could see lines and lines of 30,000 to 40,000 men, in groups of hundreds upon hundreds like cubes, formed into human boxes, standing in the main yard. So many people. A forest of people.

The Germans sent us to the showers, where they took away our clothes. Like factory parts on an assembly line, we passed through the sprinklers and received a shirt and a pair of pants on the other end. We didn't receive shoes. We went barefoot.

It was winter and cold. We were in the foothills of the mountains. They first sent us to a transit camp, a fenced-in area where we didn't work or receive food. We stayed there for three days. It was there that they assigned each of us an identification patch. They gave me a red badge, a triangle of red that signified a political/criminal prisoner. I told them I was a Jew and also received a yellow stripe. The Germans were organized bastards. Perfect order.

Out of those prisoners, I was one of the few Jews. Most of the 40,000 men were criminals, homosexuals, murderers, or professional thieves, or anyone considered to have committed crimes against Hitler. Those people had been locked up, some for fifteen to twenty years. It really was a concentration camp for German criminals against the state, not Jews specifically. In fact, until this time, none of the inmates knew I was a Jew, or even what a Jew was.

Flossenburg was a prison long before Hitler came to power. During Hitler's Reich, the prison was transformed into a concentration camp. But still, at this time, Jews weren't shipped directly to Flossenburg to be burned. We were in a slave labor camp: arms, hands, legs, and feet — work power for the Germans.

Flossenburg stood surrounded by four mountains and huge graves of people, each probably twice as large as Kibbutz Ginosar. At the transit camp, I was given a barrack number and bed. They recorded my number — the 728 tattooed on my arm in Mielec — and left it that way. Undoubtedly, Prisoner Number 728 had died, so I was granted his numerical opening.

Now in this particular camp, the blockmaster of each barrack wielded enormous power. Like a kapo, he ran the barrack, received special privileges, and because he usually had survived twenty years behind bars, he was crafty, fit, and supremely dangerous. My blockmaster was a surly man with thick forearms and a hardened face. It was his job to collect me from the transit camp and bring me to the barracks.

As a German clerk recorded my number 728, the block-master's ears perked up. He looked over at my arm and his face registered disbelief and shock. A low number, you see, afforded one the privileges of seniority — the privileges of being fed first, sleeping in the best bed, getting the prime work, and so forth. And one earned that right. The blockmaster had been at Flossenburg longer than I had been alive. He glared at me.

"This is impossible!" he raged.

He pulled my arm out for his inspection. Then he lifted up his shirtsleeve to look at his own number and dropped it again. According to his calculations, with my low number I would have to have been born in the camp, and it infuriated him. My number put a crimp in his importance and usurped his power. From such great fury at my impertinence, he slammed his fist across my face and threw me across the floor. I wasn't prepared for it. The floor was slick, slippery like ice, scrubbed and polished with sand and hot water. The barrack was clean, perfectly in order. Everything was in order, except me.

I skidded on my bottom down the aisle and hit my head against the leg of a three-tiered bunk. At that moment, I knew either he would win or I would win. I thought, *If I don't do anything, I am a dead man. If I return the same blow, I will also be a dead man.*

Remember, another law of the camp dictated that no prisoner came to the aid of another. Each man for himself. I had seconds to make a decision that would determine my fate.

The bed bunk was old. I ripped the leg off the bunk, drawing with it a long, rusty nail. With one move, I slammed the nail into that son-of-a-bitch's neck. I hit him good and hard. He collapsed, stunned. One of the other inmates drew the nail out of his neck and wrapped a rag around his throat. Finally after an hour, he got up and weaved his way over to me. Everyone stood back and stared at us, anticipating my demise.

Suddenly, the blockmaster extended his hand and shook

mine. The others continued to stare in wonder.

I didn't bend.

From that day on we were friends. I had earned his respect. And his respect meant a better bed for me, better food, better work.

The next day I went to work, and the days became routine.

CHAPTER EIGHT: Survival

I remember one discussion among us in the bunks. One of the men asked me what nationality I was. We didn't know each other by name, only by number. Or by country.

I told them, "I come from the Jewish race."

My bedmate didn't understand what that meant. Another prisoner, a reverend, occupied the bunk across the aisle. He was the barrack's resident intellectual. So they called him over and asked, "What is a Jew?"

He knew of course and answered, "You know what a Christian is? Well, this is another kind of religion, a belief." And he explained to them about the Jewish religion, impressing even me with his knowledge. But few inmates thought much more about it. And just as quickly they forgot. The government provoked anti-Semitism. These men, locked away from society for so many years, had no exposure to irrational prejudices. A man was a man based on his strength, self-worth, and work.

I'm telling you little bits and pieces of life at this camp that stick out in my mind like the odd fragments in a jigsaw puzzle of cruelty and abnormality. It is important for you to see the overall structure, the routine as it was, just as it is important for you to learn of human brutality made acceptable because of the structure. So I will describe how it was, and you'll come to some comprehension of the enormous horror of the German system and mentality.

In our block, unlike all the other camps I had lived through, we had complete order and cleanliness. Every bed had to be perfectly aligned, floors shining, clothes changed and cleaned once a week, showers taken, food divided and eaten without leaving behind one single crumb.

One of the men in the barracks, a German prisoner about forty-five years old and a professional thief, approached me. We grew to be friends as we cleaned the barracks. A man who is new to the camp always has some news to tell, an update on what is going on outside. So as we talked we slowly became trustful of each other.

He said to me, "Look, you are a young boy. I'm a grown man. If you want to survive in this hellhole, you must always remember two things: First, in this camp do not drink the water. No matter how thirsty, no matter how desperate you are, unless the water is boiled, never ever drink it. Second, when you receive food, eat every morsel, every crumb at once. When you get 120 grams of bread and one half-liter of soup, eat them on the spot. Don't save anything for the next day."

It was hard to get used to this rule, to eat everything at once — only once a day. But if you wanted to stay alive and so that your legs wouldn't collapse under you, you followed these rules.

I think in the three years at Flossenburg and later at Mauthausen, I never drank a drop of water. If I was thirsty, I didn't drink. Only the soup. And that was the most difficult of all. Because we received so little food, the men drank vats of water to fill their starving bellies, and dysentery raged through the barracks. Coupled with an outbreak of typhus, the two sicknesses caused thousands of deaths. Thousands!

It took half a year for the typhus to work its way out. In the morning I would wake up and everyone else in my bed would be dead. But it didn't bother the Germans. Everyday new transports of men were brought into the camp to replace the dead. Despite all this cleanliness, it ravaged us, this typhus. And if you didn't die from the typhus, dysentery would fell you.

One day two months later, my friend who taught me the rules of survival never returned from work.

I spent nine months in Flossenburg working on the Messerschmidt aircraft. Every chance we could get, we would try to sabotage the airplanes. When I could, I would break something in the motor and it would fall apart later when the plane was in the air. We took every opportunity to destroy these planes. But it was dangerous; if you were caught, you were hanged.

One month before I was transported out of Flossenburg, a trainload of women arrived. It was the first time in three years that I had seen a woman. I stood by the barbed wire and saw ladies and young girls coming out of a well-maintained passenger train as if they were en route to a resort, not a concentration camp. These were elegant women wearing sable coats, high heels, silks and hats, carrying leather suitcases.

Immediately the commandant ordered us to keep our eyes straight ahead. We were forbidden to move, to turn our heads and look at these women as if their presence was to remain a secret.

But I saw what happened.

The soldiers fell on them at once. There were some beautiful women coming off this train. I watched their faces change from puzzlement to slowly rising terror. The women began to shout in Czech, in Hungarian, in German, and in French as they were forced into the transport camp. I heard the German guards order, "Everyone strip!" The women took off their fancy clothes and were herded to the showers. No one comes into the camps without first going through the showers. After the showers, you are given prison clothing. But the women were left standing naked outside in the cold, open transit camp.

The Germans held them without food, water, or shelter in that transit camp for two to three weeks until each and every one of them had died. All I heard were the cries of women dying from hunger, from exposure, from beatings, rapes, tortures of the most inconceivable kinds. The crematorium pumped out smoke day after day, hour upon hour, burning those women. It was one of the hardest periods of my imprisonment, hearing the women screaming, shouting, begging all through the night. During the day we were out at work, but at night their shrieks would pierce through the camp, twisting into each and every one of us like burning knives. We men were powerless to aid them or protect them. Those women might have been our mothers, our wives, our sisters. They were all Jews. And they were killed because the Germans had nothing for them to do at the camp.

To this day, the horror of those weeks, the vision of those women, their stomachs bloated with starvation, their tongues swollen with thirst, faces and bodies distorted, lives in my memory as if it happened only yesterday.

I shall never forget it.

CHAPTER NINE: Mauthausen

One month later I was transferred with thousands of others to Mauthausen Concentration Camp,[18] a three-day cattle-train ride from Flossenburg with a two-night holdover at Auschwitz. We were given no food, no water, no exit from the boxcar.

Mauthausen was an enormous camp divided into three subcamps. Camp One, or the Central Camp, was the most orderly, holding the majority of the slave labor force, a number that reached 200,000 by 1944 and 1945. Camp Two, called Gusen I, held those workers who were becoming enfeebled or perhaps less desirable. I don't know. The third, Gusen II, was equivalent to a death sentence. Filthy, in complete disorder, Gusen II was the last and final stop. Anyone who was sent to Gusen II was either fed directly into the ovens or died before they made it to the doorway. Transport after transport was sent there. Only the strongest of men could survive it. Most of the men in Gusen II were Jews — mostly Jews from Hungary and Czechoslovakia.

In Mauthausen, I finally learned that Jews were taken and burned simply because they were Jews. In Flossenburg, up until the time I left, the Germans had only burned those who were unable to survive.

I was sent to the Central Camp.

By this time it was 1944. At Mauthausen, and even before that in Flossenburg, we began to sense that the Germans were losing the war. How did we know? When they lost on the battlefront, they would make life even more difficult for us. There were more killings, beatings, shouting, and less food. Any cruelty that would hurt us. Only from their punishments could we know when they were doing well or doing badly in the war effort. By the time I had reached Mauthausen, the Germans were doing very badly.

The first day I came to Mauthausen I stood on line for a head count and barely survived the life-and-death system called "*selektzia.*" In front of the line of incoming prisoners sat a group of "doctors" who checked us before we went into the camp. Here they weeded out the ones who were weak, sick, thin or whatever. One doctor stood holding a whip in his hand and ordered, "Left! Right! Right! Left!" as it pleased him. Everyone knew that one of these directions led to the ovens, but no one knew which one.

The area was arranged in a one-hundred-meter track. It was impossible to go off course, you see; either you went to the left or you went to the right. Understand that hundreds of us were being processed at the same time. Thousands perhaps. The whip rang out and we broke into a run — left or right.

Either I didn't understand the doctor's order or I wasn't paying attention, because I ran wildly in the direction opposite from that which the selektzia doctor ordered.

He returned me to the selection lineup.

"*Schwein*!" the doctor shouted. "Haven't you learned German yet? I said go to the right!"

The doctor whipped me soundly and then screamed, "If I said go to the right, why do you rush to the left?"

And so I ran off again, this time to the right, my behind stinging, and found myself in the Central Camp, not in the crematorium.

Mauthausen was a hellhole.

I learned that Gusen-I held the gas chambers. By 1945, the ovens couldn't keep up with the dead. When the Germans couldn't gas enough people, they lined them up and threw thousands of half-alive people into huge trenches and then poured cement on top of them. The people, still alive, squirmed under the cement. The next morning you could see ripples and ridges in the places where the men had tried to burst through. Some shapes were even standing like rock statues. It was one of the cruelest sights I have ever seen, the hardest of days. And we didn't know that liberation was only a short time away.

Before liberation, we had to continue living with the growing barbarity of the SS. The Germans liked to play games with their prisoners. One day they played a particularly memorable one called "Looking for Lice."

It was midwinter, four months before the end of the war. The Germans, as I told you, were becoming more and more brutal as they lost on more and more fronts. And we suffered their every defeat. The day the Russians crushed them on the eastern front, the SS came to us and ordered every man, thousands and thousands plus, to strip naked and then stand outside in the freezing cold.

This is how they killed lice, they said.

As we stood naked in the cold, they went through the barracks and washed the walls and floors with disinfectant. We stood outside for three days until the snow covered us or until we froze to death. Some men stood like frozen trees, their limbs stiff, encased in ice. Twenty-five percent of all the concentration-camp inmates died on the spot.

After three days, those who could still move were ordered to the showers. We had to walk over frozen bodies that were stacked up outside the showers. The shower rooms were enormous. Ten thousand men were put through at one time. After three days in the freezing cold, most fainted from the heat and steam. I saw that boiling water sprayed out of the shower nozzles. I knew then that no one could ever get out alive. With whips cracking, machine guns at our backs, the Germans ordered us through the shower assembly line. Bodies collapsed one atop the other, until there was no choice but to crawl over mountains of human limbs to come under the showerhead. I don't know why I wanted to live, but I did, so I wrapped my hand around the nozzle and held back the scalding water until I passed through to the exit. The water burned a hole through my hand – but I survived.

On the other side of the showers, they gave me back the same dirty clothes I had on three days before. It still had my number sewn on it, and they had not cleaned the clothes to remove the lice. They never intended that I would live to wear them again.

One Sunday, a short time afterward, I was working in the infamous Mauthausen quarry[19] carrying heavy stones up the 186 "Stairs of Death", as they were known, to the top of the cliff to build the ever-widening wall around the camp. On the way up the stairs, one of the cruelest of climbs, I met a boy who seemed to recognize me. I didn't know him.

We walked along together and he asked me, "Do you know that your brother Rudi just arrived at Gusen II? If you want to see him, you had better hurry because he has an infection in his hand and I don't know how much longer he will live."

His news stunned me. My eldest brother, Rudi!

I tried to imagine what Rudi looked like now. I hadn't seen him for five years. I grew determined to find a way to see him. But how to get into Gusen II?

I thought and thought about finding a way into that death camp until I hit on a plan. During roll call, men who were sick were usually sent straight to the *krankenlager* (infirmary) at Gusen II. I decided to get sick...but how? The kapos checked your body temperature, you see. It wasn't so easy.

One of the men confided, "If you want to get sick, get some cigarettes, eat them right before roll call. The tobacco will give you a fever no thermometer can measure!"

So I sold my share of bread for five cigarettes and ate them before the roll call. Within minutes, I ran a high fever. But because so many thousands were ill, by the time they came to check me, my fever had subsided. I quickly rubbed the thermometer with my thumb until the mercury had risen enough and finally they sent me off to Gusen II.

The minute I got there, I began to search for my brother.

I located his barracks and immediately asked a white-faced stick of a man if he knew him. Another half-alive corpse told me Rudi had died a few hours before and they had taken him outside the barracks to the pile of dead bodies by the fence waiting to be transported to the ovens or the trenches.

I searched through the corpses until I found my brother. I recognized him because he had the letters KL tattooed on his wrist. Those marks were given only to Jews from our area when we were imprisoned in Mielec. Round and portly Rudi, now emaciated from starvation, lay stiff like a hacked-off branch of a tree — his Steiner face, the face of my father, wasted into anonymity. It seemed that his inky tattoo KL had more life than his rigid body.

I felt nothing for this corpse. My brother. Rudi was dead and I was barely in a better situation, now stuck in the death camp of Gusen II. There I remained for one week until I thought I would die myself. Finally, the SS came to drag out those who could work, and they took me. I got a few kicks in the rear and I ran. If you can run, you can work.

So back I went to the Central Camp and to my work at the Messerschmitt airplane factory.

CHAPTER TEN: Liberation

In Mauthausen on Sundays, I worked either bringing the stones up from the quarry — a cruel, backbreaking job — or cleaning out the foul-smelling trenches used for draining the latrines. Sewage cleaning was profitable. We could find gold, aluminum, or diamonds in the waste — valuables the prisoners had swallowed to hide from the Nazis or had cached inside cylinders and held inside their rectums until dysentery hit and all types of treasures were forcibly excreted. Most people knew what could be found in those trenches. Of course the SS knew too.

Foraging through this waste one Sunday afternoon, I found a cylinder packed with gold. Thirty pieces of gold! An SS guard saw the glint of metal and knew I had found something. The packet broke open and gold fell in little pieces on the ground. He heard the ring of the metal but didn't actually see it. Immediately, I stood on the gold bits, covering them with my foot.

"Give me what you found!" the guard shouted.

I raised my head. "What do you want? I didn't find anything."

As I spoke, he hit me in the face with the butt of his revolver. He broke my nose. But I didn't give him the gold.

I could barely see. My entire face was broken, my nose shattered, which is why you see it bends to the left to this day. But the pain didn't stop me. I stood at the corner of the trench and then quickly threw the packet out toward the perimeter of the latrine, toward the fence. Either I would find it again or someone else would, but not the

SS soldier. Luckily, the SS guard didn't see me throw the packet to the wind.

That night after we showered, I returned to the corner of that same fence to look for the gold. Each gold band could buy one loaf of bread, the equivalent buying power today of twenty-five dollars. If you wanted to buy bread or cigarettes, only gold would do.

I wasn't certain I'd find the packet again. Gold digging was a hit-or-miss business, but a big business encouraged by the SS. I wasn't clever in this trade. From the gold we found, the SS would sell us bread. They made money and we ate. My hunger moved me more than my safety. It was clearly forbidden to return to the sewage trenches at night. I camouflaged my intentions by wandering around the camp like a drunk, weaving in and out of the alleys and barracks. No one paid attention to me. I burrowed through the excrement, searching, sifting for probably two hours. But I didn't find the packet.

I didn't sleep that night — my hunger for the gold was so intense. Early in the morning I returned to the sewer and, in the dawn light, I searched again. I finally decided someone had taken it. Just as I turned to head back to the barracks, I stepped on a round packet. The gold!

I had found the ten cylinders of gold right there under my foot. I was a wealthy man! I ran off with my treasure to the barracks. Eventually I bought bread. Knowing I had money to buy bread, the same SS guard beat me, broke my nose again, punched in my eyes. Ultimately most of the gold was stolen from me.

Such was life in the camps. Anything for survival.

Three weeks before the end of the war, we were already hearing Allied gunfire and bombers. One bomb fell and blew up the SS kitchen. The Germans were so busy trying to hold off the Russians, they let the Americans creep up to their doorstep. The Germans apparently decided it was preferable to fall into American hands, believing the Americans would treat them better.

The last two weeks of the war bled us. We received no food and worked nonstop, round the clock. The German attitude had changed. The SS officers had disappeared into the night and the soldiers who remained to run the camp behaved as if they had already been defeated. We saw it was going to end, but our strength to survive had been weakened by starvation. Thousands and thousands of us died during those last few weeks. So close, our freedom, so close, yet we couldn't hold on. Those of us who still clung to life, we watched as other changes took place.

A maze of tunnels led to the entrances to the underground factories. We saw that the Germans had brought in a group of explosives specialists. They worked in each factory entrance, digging holes into the stones and stuffing each hole with dynamite. At the same time, the Americans were bombing the camp from above. The bombs didn't touch us, but the Germans had a different plan. They had decided to put all the camp prisoners inside the factories and blow us all up together in one tremendous, simultaneous explosion. We could see it happening. One group of prisoners, the electricians, watched the Germans with practiced eyes. The electricians knew that in order to blow us up, the Germans would first have to push the button of an electrified charger. Two days before liberation, the electricians sabotaged the entire system by cutting all the charged wires to all the tunnel entrances.

The dynamite didn't go off.

As for the electricians, I never saw them again.

That last day we knew something major had occurred because our shift worked six hours longer than we should have. We waited for the next shift to replace us, and waited and waited. Apparently the Germans had planned to blow up both shifts together. The shift changed, but the second group never came. We were so far removed from the outside world, working so deeply hidden underground in the Messerschmitt factory that no one knew the Americans had reached the camp's boundaries.

Suddenly the factory went black.

During the hour-long power outage, the German SS officers disappeared. When the lights came on, 40,000 prisoners in our shift ran for the tunnel exits. Chaos, panic and a sweeping urge for freedom ensued, one person trampling over the other. You can't possibly comprehend how many bodies raced over each other to the exits. I didn't understand what was going on. I just thought the electricity had gone out, but when I also reached the outside, comprehension slowly filtered through that liberation had finally come to Mauthausen.

What I saw outside shocked me to a full stop.

Thousands upon thousands of inmates lay hanging from the camp boundary fences, burnt to a crisp from the electricity still surging through the barbed wire. Yet more and more kept running like wild animals toward the fences, running to freedom but meeting death. Wave upon wave of prisoners stampeding forward toward the electrified fences, forcing all those ahead of them in the direction of the fences. Death met them before they even reached the wires. Six feet away from the fence, prisoners fleeing to freedom were jolted to death as they came in contact with the charged bodies of the thousands who had fallen before them.

I saw more people killed that day than at any other time. Thousands! The time was four o'clock in the afternoon, May 5, 1945. I shall never forget the date. Even the weather — rainy, raw, and cold — burdened our liberation on this spring afternoon by churning the ground we pounded in our flight into a tragic, muddy, nightmarish finale to the Holocaust.

I raced back to the barracks. The inmates had set fire to block after block. Flames roared through the wooden huts. The camp turned into an inferno. Everything was ablaze. I didn't help the others raze the rest of the camp. While hundreds of blocks burned, I ran to search for food. The heat was intense. For the first time in five years,

I wasn't cold.

Grabbing a bucket, I ran off to search for potatoes behind the soldiers' barracks. I wasn't alone. Thousands, literally thousands of other prisoners were scraping the earth. I returned to the blazing barracks and threw the potatoes, still caked with mud, into a pail of water. I don't think I bothered to wait for the water to boil. I was too starved. I ate the whole bucketful, a full bucket of raw potatoes, just like that.

All that night we stayed awake with excitement. As our prison burned to the ground around us, we sat outside talking, planning, wondering how to get out, where to go. In a sense, I suppose we felt like orphaned children. We didn't think about anything but filling our stomachs — food, food, just to eat and fill our stomachs with food. But it was also chilly. We wore threadbare clothing. I cut a pair of leather boots off a dead soldier. I had walked barefoot for years.

The next morning I saw my first American soldier when I ran past the main gates to look for food. Converging on the entrance were American tanks lined up 100 meters[20] abreast. While everyone else was running to the main gates to look at the Americans, I was running to the fields to look for food.

That same day, I saw the SS standing in lines, one by one, handing their weapons to the Americans. The whole camp blazed well into the morning. The smoke of burning wood blanketed the stench of the hundreds of thousands of dead bodies that littered the trenches, the ground, and the fences.

At one point we began to hear rumors that it was safe to go out of the camp, although some SS were still on the road ambushing prisoners, killing and shooting. We organized a group of fifteen to twenty men and walked out the main gate. No one stopped us. I tell you, it was a day of complete and utter chaos.

My comrades and I found our way to Linz, a city divided in half by a river. On the bridge, we saw a huge contingent of American soldiers leading a group of SS captives to a prisoner-of-war camp. We wanted to catch a few of them for ourselves. We waited an hour or so to figure out how to grab them, but most of us were weak and it proved difficult.

Heavily guarded by a unit of black American soldiers, the POWs passed by us on the bridge. I remember that the soldiers were black because I had never seen a black man before. As if it was our right, we asked the soldiers for their weapons to take a few German Nazis for ourselves. I don't think you should know this — it wasn't something the Americans would want to publicize — but the soldiers gave us their bayonets and we ran into those SS prisoners, piercing their bodies, skewering them like raw meat, then tossed those we could over the bridge into the river. The rest we piled up on the bridge. We killed so many of those Nazi SS that afternoon that you couldn't pass over the bridge anymore.

We were there a good few hours until an American officer finally came, closed access to the bridge, and took us all off to a detention camp. It didn't take us long to cut our way out of their simple barbed-wire fencing. We returned immediately to Linz.

We wandered around the city for a full day and night, looking for food along with many thousands of other prisoners from the camps. The Germans fled. The Americans came. We slept on the sidewalks after finding clean, warm clothes that we looted from kiosks or deserted stores.

That next morning, a truck filled with American soldiers stopped and gave us a lift. We took off with them, my comrades and I, without any sense of direction and found ourselves in Salzburg, Austria. I remember it as a beautiful, ancient city. We wandered around for two or three days in the streets. The Germans and Austrians were afraid of us. We did things I'm not proud of today, but then we needed to do those things — to kill and rape, to take everything and anything we wanted. We were wild, uncivilized animals, men-children of the camps, men-children of a beastly nightmare living by instinct, cunning, hatred, and revenge.

One afternoon I caught a glimpse of a soldier with a Star of David on his epaulet. It stunned me. I watched him closely and read the words "British Brigade" encircling the star. I couldn't believe a Jew existed on this earth, alive, a soldier, not a prisoner. I followed him about the city. I couldn't let him out of my sight. Finally after he sat himself down by a statue in the city square, I approached him. Closer now, I saw the word "Palestine" embroidered on his badge.

I asked him in German, "Are you from Palestine?"

"Are you Jewish?" he answered in Yiddish.

"Yes," I said.

"What are you doing here in Salzburg? You should go to Palestine," he told me.

I asked him how to get there.

He explained that I must go to Italy with the army convoys and when I got there, I'd find a way to Palestine by first finding the Haganah. The Haganah was the Jewish paramilitary branch of the British Army and was now organizing immigration, legal and illegal, into Palestine for every refugee and Jewish inmate of Hitler's camps. I didn't know much about Palestine. I saw only that here was a healthy, free soldier wearing a Star of David, a Jew from Palestine. I wanted to be there as well.

Immediately I organized a group of twelve comrades to go to Italy.

Three days later we came to the Italian border at Brenna. Our train was so overloaded with ex-prisoners that the twelve of us had to climb up and sit on the roof. When we arrived in Rome, we were seven. Two men had fallen off when the train swerved around a cliff, and the electric cables along the tracks had electrocuted three others when we passed through a mountain tunnel. Yet I remember only how we were starving. And how the Italian soldiers shared their sausages with us, passing them up to the roof from their open windows into our outstretched hands. I ate my first olive on board that train and got a small jolt from the taste. Funny, now I love them.

At Rome we didn't know where to get off. The station stops went on forever. When we'd ask where Rome was, everyone would point here, there. In fact, because the station was so big, we walked around the train depot for two days. We thought all of Rome was one train station.

How did we survive without money or shelter? We broke into kiosks to get food. We slept on benches. We stole. We ransacked or raided any place we came across. I spent my first three months of freedom in Rome wandering around, eating everything I could find, taking women, stealing clothes, living without fear. We never thought of tomorrow.

After five years in camps, I didn't know anything about women. But in Rome you woke up fast. I felt wild, like an animal. For a long time I slept on the floor; I couldn't get comfortable on a bed. My hair took its time growing in. I still had the shaved *"autostrada"* stripe down the middle of my scalp. My face and nose had healed, but those raw strips of flesh on my backside never came right.

I didn't find any Jewish Palestinians in Rome. By then I had forgotten about that meeting in Salzburg. I just looked for a good time. I knew my parents and brothers were dead — Rudi in Mauthausen, and Willi had died in Flossenburg in 1944. I learned this from someone I met in Mauthausen, who told me he heard the SS had come to our farm shortly after my arrest. First they shot the dog, he said. Then they shot my parents. I had no one left, so I didn't think further about finding a family. That part of me — the young boy from a farm in Poland, from a big family in Gromnik — had died years before. I was completely alone.

CHAPTER ELEVEN: Rome

After I had enough of the easy life in Rome (really, no one can ever have enough), I went to work as a truck driver for the American army, which issued me identification papers. I told them I had an uncle in the States, even though I could remember no more than that. Your grandfather Solomon, you know, his name had fallen far back in my memory. But I wanted work, so I used my American connection.

To tell you the truth, I really had no idea if any part of my family lived in America and couldn't have cared less. But a strange thing happened. One afternoon, after I had come back from making a delivery, an American officer with whom I had made friends called for me over the loudspeaker in the garage where I worked.

"Do you have a relative named Solomon Steiner in New Jersey?" he asked me when I entered his office.

"Yes," I said, not knowing if I had one or not, not even knowing where New Jersey was. It sounded like the right thing to say.

I remember how the officer sat down and put his feet up on the desk, looking very pleased.

"Well, it's a funny thing," he said. "I was down at the docks today and they were unloading jeeps from the States. One of the jeeps had a sticker on the back saying a certain Solomon Steiner of Newark, New Jersey, donated it to the army. I had to scratch my head. That's not such a common name. I thought maybe it could be your relative. What a coincidence!"

The officer had felt sorry for me from the first day we met. He was anxious to help me find family.

"I'll wire him and verify your relationship. We'll have an answer in twenty-four hours."

I'm sure I looked uninterested because, in fact, I couldn't really remember much about my father's family after five years in the camps, not to mention an old uncle, one of my father's many brothers, who left Poland for America when I was a child. I couldn't even remember being a child.

Within two days, the officer received a reply from Solomon himself verifying that he was indeed my uncle and that he would send passage money for me to come to America. In the meantime, I was to organize papers.

I was surprised. America? I couldn't comprehend what that meant. I only knew Rome. I was eighteen years old. It really didn't make much difference to me whether I stayed here or went there. As long as I had food — that was all that mattered.

Nevertheless, in due course a ticket arrived for passage on an ocean liner sailing to New York from Naples. The evening before my departure, I sat for the last time with some of my friends drinking at a coffee house. My bags were packed. Rather, my one satchel with some clothes I had collected since my attachment to the Americans had been left in my room at a local *pensionne*, packed and waiting for me to pick it up before the ship left in the morning.

Just as I was about to drink a shot of whiskey, someone I had never seen before came up to me, pointed his fingers in my face and said, "You! Your name is Steiner. You had three brothers — Rudi, Willi, and Poldek."

I looked back into his old, broken face. I didn't recognize him. But he remembered me very well indeed. We had worked together in Mielec three years before. He had slept two tiers below me in our barrack's bunk.

As I came to understand who this man was, he continued talking and said, "Do you know your brother Poldek is alive?"

I stared at him incredulously.

The old man told me he and Paul were freed together from Mauthausen.

I hadn't even known my brother and I were in the same camp.

He went on to add that the two of them decided to return to Poland to search for family. They never got there. Poland was a dangerous place after the war. Jews were still being murdered in the countryside and cities. Because they had difficulties crossing the border into Poland, they ended up in Czechoslovakia instead. There, they registered with the Joint[21] in case a surviving relative was trying to locate them. Then Poldek, or Paul as he later came to be known, my ambitious older brother, opened up a sewing factory with start-up money from the Jewish Agency. Because business was too good and because he was comfortable, Paul wanted to stay where he was. After a time, this man left Paul behind in Czechoslovakia and went off to find his way to Palestine. So he returned through Germany before the borders proved impassable and then moved on to Italy to find his way onto an Aliyah Bet boat, which is how he came to see me waiting to board the ship to America at the port in Naples.

There was no question in my mind about what I had to do.

I got up from the table, dropped my whiskey into someone else's hand and left Naples. I left everything behind with a friend — my clothes, my identification papers, my money, my ship's passage to New York. I only returned to the pensionne to dress warmly for the long journey to Prague.

That same night I took a train north toward Germany. When the train approached the Italian/German border, I jumped off and crossed the Alps on foot. It took twelve hours to get across the border. I finally arrived in Munich two days later. There I went to search for people I knew who could help me cross into Czechoslovakia. It wasn't a simple thing to do, going into a Communist country. I needed help.

I met a friend who made inquiries and found how I could maneuver my way across the Czech border. But that is another story for another book.

I managed to get into Czechoslovakia without getting caught. I was shot at by border guards, hid out in empty train cars, traded my cigarettes for train tickets and food, weaved through a hundred checkpoints until I arrived in Prague weeks later.

I searched for my brother for three or four days, perhaps even a week. I couldn't find him. I searched in every office, in every neighborhood, in every business district until I became thoroughly depressed. There wasn't anyone I could share my problem with. I felt such a great sorrow, such a letdown not to be able to find my brother. Here I had risked my life, traveled dangerously, crossed borders illegally, climbed over mountains, evaded bullets, all for nothing.

From Naples to Prague, the entire trip took at least a month and a half, a trip of constant checkpoints, border guards, soldiers and secret police, checking all the time. You had to find every possible way to slip out of their hands. No, it wasn't an easy trip. If I had any concept of what awaited me on this journey, I wonder if I would have made this attempt.

After yet another day wandering around the streets searching for Paul, I started to feel angry. I thought, *Why do I have to look for him? Let him come and look for me!* Here I had done everything, made supreme efforts to find him...and for nothing. If Paul wanted to find me, I decided, it was his turn to look. I gave up right then and walked directly to the train station.

"Now," I said, "I am going back to Italy. I will look no further."

Weeks later, having retraced all the steps that took me from country to country, I finally got off the train and once again I was back in Munich.

The first thing on my mind was food. I headed straight for a restaurant at the station, sat down, and ordered a bowl of steaming soup. Just as I lifted the first spoonful to my mouth, I hadn't even swallowed yet, a man approached the table and announced, "You, Yonah Steiner! Do you know your brother is alive?"

Here I had just sat down to eat. For days I hadn't eaten. I was exhausted and hungry. The only thing I looked forward to was a hot meal and a cold beer. Yet this man persisted. He drew a chair out from under my table, sat himself down, and shook my arm.

"Do you know your brother is alive?" he asked again.

"Which brother?" I shook his arm free.

"Your brother, Paul. *Poldek.*"

I stared at him as if he were an idiot. My soup was getting cold.

"I just came from Czechoslovakia," he told me. "I saw your brother Paul."

As it turned out, we had both just traveled from the Czech border to Munich on the same train. This man, who apparently recognized me from one of our camp imprisonments, went on to explain that Paul was definitely alive and working in Czechoslovakia, but he was not in Slovakian Prague. I had been mistaken. Paul lived in the Czech city of Bratislava.

It was ten o'clock in the evening. I knew at four in the morning another train would make the return trip to the border. What to do? I no longer had any money. I was completely out of food. I was tired. Exhausted. Everything was gone. I had no cigarettes left to trade. I sat at the café table until three o'clock in the morning trying to make up my mind.

I decided to go back.

I had fewer problems reaching Prague this time. Once there, I caught a train to Bratislava. I bought off the guards at Bruno with cigarettes I had stolen, and slipped into the Communist section of the country without difficulty.

A day later, I was in Bratislava.

I searched for Paul a good week. Bratislava is no small town. There were many people moving about, shifting from one place to the next, so it was difficult to find anyone who knew about his neighbor. One night, almost at my wits' end, I came across an office that posted refugee listings. I could see the man in charge sleeping in the back room. I banged on the door until he got out of bed. Through the curtained window I saw him pull a gun from the top drawer of a cabinet and approach the door.

He opened the door cautiously. He was a swarthy-looking Czech, black hair, pockmarked skin. I told him I wanted to have a look in the files. He stared at me as if I was mad to wake him. I didn't care what he thought. I was tired and fed up.

He raised the gun and pointed it at me. "The office is closed," he snarled. "Get out of here, *Yid*. You should have burned with the rest of them!"

I slammed him against the wall with such force I nearly killed him. The gun fell from his hand. I picked it up and brought the muzzle to his face.

"I'll kill you first," I threatened, "but before I do, open the files. I'm looking for someone."

Holding his head in his hand, he struggled to the cabinets. He twisted a key in the lock and waited.

"*Steiner, Leopold,*" I ordered.

The Czech shuffled through the papers, but they were in total disorder. Not one file was arranged in alphabetical order, as it should have been.

I threw open all the file drawers and dumped each bulging box of papers on the floor.

"I don't care if it takes the whole night. You're going to go through each file from A to Z until you find my brother's name!"

I could easily have killed him. It would have been a pleasure. But first there was work to do. We searched every paper, every piece of writing within each and every file—every scrap, every note, every scribble.

But after three hours, we found nothing. Absolutely nothing. Paul Steiner, Leopold Steiner, Poldek Steiner did not exist. I left the Czech sitting on the floor amid the massive pile of papers and manila office folders. I threw his gun across the room and stalked out. My despair was second only to my anger.

The next morning I continued my search. I was too angry to give up. I roamed through an industrial area of the city until I found myself in front of a textile factory. It must have been eight o'clock in the morning. I opened the front door, stepped into the anteroom and peered through another door, this one made of beveled glass, to have a look at the huge workroom humming with the sound of dozens of sewing machines.

I opened the glass door and stared hard into the face of each and every worker, row upon row of heads bent down to their sewing machines in the factory. The one face I was looking for I didn't see.

Either I pulled the door behind me too fast, or in frustration I slammed it too hard, I don't know why, but the door shut with such force that the huge pane of glass shattered into a thousand pieces.

The noise stunned everyone.

An office door snapped open and a man stuck his head out to see what had happened. I looked at him. He was shorter than I and wore finely tailored clothes. He had a brush of curly dark hair swept back from his forehead. Seeing him gave me a shock. I made my way to his office. Ignoring the other people in the room, I walked over and stood directly in front of him.

"Do you know who I am?" I asked in Yiddish.

He shook his head.

"Isn't there something familiar about my face?"

He growled at me impatiently, furious about the broken door.

"Who the hell are you? I've never seen you before in my life!"

"Well, that's strange," I said. "Because I know you. I know your name, where you're from, who your parents are. And still you don't know who I am?"

He looked back at me with great irritation.

"Well, then, do you at least know your brother Yonah is alive?"

His mouth dropped. "No. I didn't know," he said, emotion creeping into his voice. "Where is he?"

I stepped back so he could take a better look. "I'm your brother. I'm your brother Yonah."

CHAPTER TWELVE: Czechoslovakia

Paul turned white with shock, and then the blood rushed back into his face as the excitement penetrated. He grabbed me and hugged me to him, unable to speak. Tears rolled down my brother's cheeks. He almost fainted from emotion. My brother. I had no such reaction. After all, I knew who he was and knew he was alive. If anything, I felt almost irritated that it took him so long to recognize me.

I don't believe I had any personal feelings that morning. The five years in the camps were still too fresh in my mind. Actually, I think I hadn't felt any emotion for many years. Nothing affected me, neither physical pain nor emotional horror. Nothing moved me. I was unable to cry. Even today I cannot cry. It's difficult. I just cannot explain my feelings to you. It's something buried, clogged up, cut out, closed up forever. The truth is, my feelings, or rather my inability to feel is not a normal thing. I know this hasn't happened to every person who went through what I did. I feel to this day that I am not a normal person. There are only a few situations in which I'm sensitive — situations that take me into a deep and almost abnormal sorrow. Most of the time it doesn't matter what has happened; I am completely closed. My feelings do not exist. I think it's from...I don't know how to explain it.

I used to think that there were many people who didn't have emotions. It's not always that way with me. Today I'm more sensitive, more feeling. Once I was like stone. I never thought of tomorrow. I never wanted to have a lot of anything. What I had was enough. I only took care that there would continue to be enough. After the war, I had enough of everything. I had money. I lived it up. I never looked at tomorrow or thought of tomorrow. Today I am alive. Today I eat what I want, as much as I want. I never think even one hour ahead.

On the other hand, Paul's feelings and way of life were much different. We were not built the same. First of all, he was highly emotional. He cried. He remembered how to cry. And he hugged me. I didn't know how to respond. We sat in his office, his hand on mine, and we talked and talked. Paul had been in the camps for four years, the last year in Mauthausen, until he escaped a few weeks before liberation.

"I only wanted to kill," Paul told me. "I only wanted to kill and kill Germans until there were no bullets or no blood left."

He had joined a British brigade and received a rifle. Then he went on a killing spree that lasted one month. An accident stopped his rampage. Paul fell into a ravine and cracked his head on a stone. When he woke up he found himself in a Red Cross hospital, only he had no memory of who he was or where he came from. My brother Poldek lived with this amnesia for three months until one day he came to remember all that had happened — the ghosts of the camps, the nightmares that were his life. He remembered that he was Paul Steiner. At that moment, he told me, all his rage was replaced by an obsessive need for security and a home. He set off for Poland to see if any of us remained alive. Then, unable to cross the border, he went south into Czechoslovakia.

Now I sat opposite him in his office. He had done well, my brother. He ran a big factory with many employees. But his status didn't move me in the slightest.

"Look," I said to him after he had recovered from the shock of seeing me, "I've come to take you away with me. You are not staying here."

My plans were to return to Italy and from Italy to go on to the United States or, even better, to Palestine. I always had it in my head not to remain in the Diaspora but to return to a land that belonged to the Jews. At that moment, I had completely forgotten about Uncle

Solomon and his ticket.

"Listen," I told him, "I see you have a big thing here. It's very nice, but forget it. You're coming with me."

Paul looked at me in shock.

"But," he said, "I can't leave everything behind like this. This business is worth a lot of money. It took me months to build up what I have."

I reminded him at once, "Our parents also had a lot, and because of that they are not alive today. And all our family had a lot. Now there is no one. Poldek, what is left from all of our family, from all that we know, is just you and me. I tell you this now, let's get out of here. The sooner the better."

I was willing to move right then. Nothing was in my way. Paul went to speak with his workers and told them that after lunch he would be giving me a lift to the train station and would not be back until the next day.

I told Paul to forget it. He was coming with me. Not only was he coming with me, he was also leaving everything behind. Everything — taking only what was already in his pockets and the clothes on his back.

"The hell with it all!" I shouted at him. "You don't need any of this. Come with me now!"

Paul reluctantly agreed.

He instructed his workers what to cut and sew for the next day and then, returning to me in the office, said, "What's your hurry? Rest a few days. Let's organize some money and clothes."

I wouldn't budge. There was a train out of the city that evening and we would be on it. My brother didn't have a choice. But I did agree to eat lunch. We sat and had a meal in his office while we waited for one of his workers to secretly purchase two tickets for that evening's train.

So with our stomachs full and two tickets in our hands, we

got up to leave. Paul wavered for a fifth time, trying to convince me to stay. Exasperated, I took the office keys from his pocket, smacked them into his secretary's fist and, before all their stunned faces, pushed my brother out to the anteroom and pulled what was left of the glass door shut behind us.

And that was that.

Paul and I traveled back the same route, struggled on foot across the Czech/German border and arrived in Munich a month later. By now it was winter and the first snows had fallen. The pass through the Alps was buried in snow. We could not get through to Italy.

We decided to stay in Germany until spring.

CHAPTER THIRTEEN: Hamburg

Paul and I needed to look for work.

Paul found a small room and again opened up a tailor shop in Munich. He did very well. I didn't know what to do until I heard about a navigation school that was opening in Hamburg, sponsored by the Haganah. I decided to go and study there until spring, when Paul and I could continue to Italy.

In the Hamburg school, I learned fishing, navigation and ship mechanics. That's also where I met Rivkah, who had come to Bergen-Belsen to look for her family. Regina (Rivkah) Zinger had come from a small village in the Ukraine called Medyn but had managed to survive the war years disguised as a Polish Catholic farm girl. She had been working in Germany on the farm of an SS officer's family, and when liberation came was afraid to tell them she was really Jewish. It took her a good couple of months to admit the truth. But Rivkah has her own story. You must talk to her and she will tell you how she came to survive when all the rest of her family were murdered. And you see — that is why we came together, just like that. We'd both lost our families. We both wanted a family.

So my plans began to solidify. We decided to get married and went back together to Munich to see Paul. He, in the meantime, began to get too involved with business again. He also met a French woman named Collette.* Paul wanted to go to France with her and get married. She told him he could do even better in Paris and he decided to give it a try. Collette wasn't Jewish. We argued about her. I told him to leave her and come with Rivkah and me to Palestine. He was a Jew. That's where he belonged. That's where all Jews belonged. The argument went on for days.

"I don't care anymore what I am!" shouted Paul. "I don't want to be a Jew if it means such suffering. I don't care about Palestine. I'm tired and fed up. I'm going to settle down and do it my own way."

My brother was a real Steiner. Stubborn.

So our plans to go on to Palestine or even the United States faded away. Your Grandpa Solomon was all but forgotten. I decided to help Paul get to France and sent for my money from my room in Naples via a friend. I gave Paul all I had. With identity papers organized, he left for Paris with Collette and I returned to Hamburg with Rivkah, now my wife.

You must understand one thing: after the war, after such terrible dislocation, those of us who survived groped toward each other to replace families we had lost. Hundreds of thousands of refugees like me, like Rivkah, would meet a woman or man and be married two days later. That's how we connected to civilization again, rebuilt our lives again. I knew Rivkah no longer than two weeks. She had lost her entire family. We became each other's only link to life. I could understand my brother's desire to settle in one place and build a family. We had lost everything, every security known to a human being.

I couldn't blame Paul, but your Grandpa Solomon did. We had one last communication with him. I believe we let him know our change of plans. Paul wrote that he had married. Uncle Solomon was furious that Collette was not Jewish and cut Paul off without another word.

He was also furious with me for deciding to go to Palestine rather than to the United States. I never knew Uncle Solomon. Only vaguely, somewhere in the memories of my lost childhood could I recall his visit. He meant nothing to me. He wasn't my father. He couldn't replace my mother or brothers. I forgot him.

I wrote Uncle Solomon only one time more, a few years later when I reached Palestine and it became the State of Israel, to ask for some socks and food because we were so poor then and Rivkah had just given birth to Shimone, our first son. We didn't have enough to eat.

The country was suffering a massive economic depression. Uncle Solomon never answered me then.[22] I don't want to hear from him now. It's too late. He turned his back on me because I wouldn't go to America. He wrote off Paul because he married a gentile. What did your rich grandfather know about the camps? We made it without his money. I don't need it today. And until you came here to Kibbutz Ginosar eighteen years later looking for the Steiner whose name is written on the return address of an old envelope, I had all but forgotten about this so-called family of mine in America.

CHAPTER FOURTEEN: Cyprus

But I am making a detour.

So how did I finally end up in Israel, you keep asking? That, too, was no simple task.

After the navigation school term ended, Rivkah and I decided it was time to make our way to Palestine. First we traveled to Belgium, where Rivkah received a Jewish Agency certificate to go to Palestine legally. She held a German passport and therefore was a citizen of someplace. But most of us were men and women without countries. I received a certificate because I was married to her. The Jewish Agency representatives in Europe issued only a small number of certificates and thousands of people wanted them. I gave up my certificate to another girl. I had my reasons. First, I wanted to pass through Italy again; and second, I knew I could get to Palestine by my own wiles, whereas women would have a more difficult time.

Seven friends from the navigation school also accompanied us to Belgium. They were also waiting for passes into Palestine. I promised my friends I would personally get them into Palestine, all seven of them, if they would come back with me to Italy.

Rivkah and I were married only one week when we went our separate ways. She went to Palestine on a boat from Marseilles. My seven friends and I went off to Italy. Because we lacked identity papers, we had lots of problems along the route and it took months before we saw Naples.

We had already made a connection with the Haganah in our

school in Hamburg. The Haganah set up a network of Palestinian Jews who would help route refugees to Israel. Our responsibility was to reach a certain port in Italy and catch up with an Aliyah Bet ship. Aliyah Bet was the Haganah's term for illegal immigration. You see, the British ran Palestine. They didn't want any more Jews to come there and upset the population balance with the Arabs. The Arabs were putting pressure on the British, and the British didn't exactly love the Jews, so the Palestinian Jews took the matter into their own hands.

At the port, we met many Palestinian Jews who worked under false names and with false papers, and whose primary purpose was to get as many Jews out of Europe and through the British blockade as they could. They guided us to old, junked boats we were to repair or skipper. I worked on the *Exodus* before it even had a name.

Four times I went to sea on these barely seaworthy vessels to bring Jewish refugees into Palestine, and four times I never reached the shore. In the middle or toward the end of each trip, once the ship was safely under way, the Palestinians would pull me off the boat and ferry me back to Italy to help prepare another tub for the next voyage.

On the fourth trip, I decided I had had enough of good deeds. I was going all the way this time. My seven comrades, who were still with me, agreed.

We were transporting six hundred and fifty children on this particular ship. As we approached the coast of Palestine, the British opened fire on the barge, boarded us, and sent those of us who didn't try to swim to shore and weren't caught straight to British detention camps in Cyprus.

Why didn't we fight the British to keep them from boarding our ship, you ask? We couldn't. There were too many children aboard whose lives were at stake. We had no choice but to surrender. They were armed. We were not.

Caught by the British, I found myself once again a prisoner. I felt sick to see another camp, another camp teeming with poor, sick

Jewish refugees. However it was impossible to compare the British detention camps with the German concentration camps. The Cyprus detention camps were simply holding pens for unwanted refugees, not death chambers.

For the first few days it felt so strange. *What's this*? *What are these barbed wires*? I found it hard to comprehend that I was locked behind a stockade patrolled by British soldiers — a prisoner again.

In any event, by the second night in the camp, I found an easy way out. My escape was so simple it was almost laughable. We burrowed under a strip of the barbed wire behind the latrines, and once on the other side, we brushed ourselves off and ambled into Famagusta to have a drink at a local coffee house. I ate well, had a good time. But I was still stuck on an island filled with British soldiers, and it wasn't simple to escape their patrols after curfew. In the early morning hours when they closed the restaurant, I wandered out to the street. At that very moment, an army jeep passed by and two soldiers grabbed me and sent me back to the camp.

So we decided to make an official escape, my seven comrades and I. We spent our nights digging a deeper tunnel through the back garbage dumps, a tunnel that would exit far beyond the perimeters of the camp. I also spent a good many evenings slipping away into Famagusta. I got to know the city very well. I lacked nothing. I even received a package of clothes and cigarettes from Rivkah who was now settled on Kibbutz Ein Gev. She had no idea how I was living it up in Famagusta.

It took six weeks to finish the tunnel. Those of us who had worked together on the ships slid out through the tunnel during the night — a group of fifteen, including my seven friends who started this journey with me in Belgium. We slipped into the port of Famagusta, stole a small dinghy, and pushed off into the dark Mediterranean Sea. Imagine! Here we were, fifteen men rowing for three days on the open sea without any idea where we were heading. We had no compass. We didn't even have a motor. Just oars. We had no water, no food.

Luck came our way in the form of a Turkish freighter. They passed us on the sea, saw we were floundering, and took us aboard. They brought us to the coast of Palestine near Herzliya. The British weren't looking for a Turkish freighter with a handful of Jews.

We landed safely on the beach that same night.

CHAPTER FIFTEEN: Israel

Don't ask me how I felt. The minute our legs hit the beach we took off. Anywhere was good enough. We were home. Eretz Israel! Home of the Jews.

We found ourselves on the shores of Kibbutz Galei Yam. A kibbutznik directed us to the Jewish Agency, which had set up a small refugee operations camp nearby. At the camp, I asked how to get to Ein Gev. At this point, the seven friends I promised to bring to Israel were still with me. My friends agreed to go on with me until I reached Rivkah, a long bus ride to the northern Galilee and a boat ride across the Kinneret to her kibbutz settlement of Ein Gev.

In the morning we found the bus to Tiberias and set out.

What were my first impressions of Israel? I had none. Nothing interested me about it. I only cared to get to where I had planned to go. Ein Gev. Only Ein Gev. I didn't care about anything else. Nothing else was important. My wife was waiting for me on a kibbutz. What a kibbutz was I had no idea. I only knew that when I got there I would then think about the next step.

A year had passed since our separation in Hamburg. It was now January 1947. Our armored bus took us only as far as Tiberias and then an armored Haganah lorry brought us down to Kibbutz Degania where we boarded a kibbutz fishing boat and crossed the Sea of Galilee (Kinneret) to Ein Gev. No one traveled around the lake by road.[23] In fact, there there wasn't even a road to Ein Gev in those days. It was too dangerous to build one. Arab marauders ambushed travelers who went by land. Even the *Egged* bus that rolled down the mountain into Tiberias was armored.

When I saw Tiberias and the Sea of Galilee below, nothing registered in my mind. To me, Tiberias was the town on the shore of the Sea of Galilee only as a place where people were living. The palm trees, the mountains, the blue sea and tropical vegetation, the beauty didn't even penetrate.

Finally we reached Ein Gev. I, Yonah Steiner, and my seven friends. We kept our word. We lived. We survived. We reached home.

Someone directed us to a group of huts. It was late in the afternoon and Rivkah was resting in her tiny little *tzrif*, a tin shack no bigger than a water closet. I didn't go inside first. Instead, I sent each of our seven friends through the door, one at a time, until there was no room left for another soul.

I could hear Rivkah's voice cry out in surprise. She probably thought, *Everyone is here but Yonah. Where is he?*

Then I went in.

And so my life began again as a kibbutznik on Ein Gev in that tiny tzrif. Rivkah and I shared a single bed and an orange crate for our work clothes. It was enough.

I had always planned to leave the kibbutz, to build a house. But fate changed my plans. The only move we made was across the lake to Kibbutz Ginosar in 1951 because of a political division among the members in Ein Gev. But even before that move, I began to meet people, to work in the kibbutz garage building irrigation pipelines and machinery and, most important, weapons for the war that was about to erupt.

I quickly learned Hebrew because no one would speak to me in any other language. The inability to communicate depressed me in the beginning. I wanted to speak in Yiddish or German, even Polish. But no one listened. No one would speak to me unless I spoke Hebrew.

In the end it was the fastest way to learn. That's why I said the same to you. And, you see, in six month's time you know Hebrew and you know my story.

PART II:
RECONCILIATION

CHAPTER SIXTEEN: Reconciliation

Yonah's story created a determination in me to unite my grandfather with his brother's son after forty years of nonrecognition.

And so a great miracle happened here.

In 1973, the third year of my Israeli sojourn, my grandfather, Solomon Steiner, packed up his bags and brought himself and my grandmother, Rose Lichtstein Steiner, to Israel to live — and to die. My stubborn and proud grandfather at the age of eighty-three had met his match with his just as stubborn and proud nephew, Yonah Steiner.

The two grew inseparable during my grandfather's remaining years. Yes, they argued about care packages of socks that never arrived or arrived but didn't get there, about boat tickets that were left in a drawer in Naples. About Paul marrying a French Catholic woman. They argued about the kibbutz not keeping kosher, about the sacrilegious lack of a synagogue within walking distance. About building a *shul* on Ginosar so my grandparents could live in this Garden of Eden.

Yonah laughs when he recounts how he first tried to pry my grandfather away from his Tel Aviv hotel for his first visit to the kibbutz to enjoy Rivkah's hospitality. My grandfather, certain that he and my grandmother would be taken to a barren desert, protested loudly and told the hotel clerk they were not checking out. In order to convince them to make the trip north to the Galilee, Yonah promised to drive them all the way back to Tel Aviv the very same night. A promise he kept, even though it meant a three hour drive twice in the same day.

"His eyes popped out of his head when he saw the kibbutz," Yonah nods as he remembers the day with nostalgia. "He couldn't believe how beautiful and green Ginosar was. And the Kinneret, the gardens, the flowers — he thought he had fallen into paradise right then and there!"

And so it came to be, forty years late, but not too late, that the Steiner family embraced each other with hands that by this time trembled from a shared palsy, a handshake between Yonah and my grandfather Solomon that brought two lost and wandering families back together from opposite sides of the ocean.

My grandfather Solomon became not only a father to Yonah, but also a grandfather to Yonah's three sons — Shimone, Avi, and Amit. Yonah represented the last living link to my grandfather's world, a world Solomon's own American-born children and grandchildren never knew and would never know: a Jewish Poland forever banished, the memories of a time, place, and family buried under a mountain of ash. My grandfather represented the same and more to Yonah. He restored a family to his brother's son.

When my grandfather died, his passing left a void in all of our lives. Yet Yonah talks of *HaZaken*, the Old Man, with a wry smile on his face. Wasted years? Wasted anger? I think so. But seeing Yonah smile as he speaks of my grandfather erases the pain, and I know that he knows he is not, nor will he ever again be, alone or forsaken.

PART III:
THE
RETURN

CHAPTER SEVENTEEN: Origins

The Steiner genes are very strong.

Although the Nazis killed six million Jews in the Holocaust more than sixty years ago, they didn't erase all of us. My grandfather Solomon, who died in 1980, lived to be almost ninety. My grandmother Rose died at ninety-six. When this chapter was first written in 2006, my own father had just celebrated his eighty-sixth birthday. Today he is eighty-eight. His younger brother, my uncle David, seventy-eight in 2006, is now just a few months shy of age eighty, and hasn't slowed down a bit. My father's older sister, Aunt Elsie, despite personal tragedies that would fell the strongest of the strong, remains a force to be reckoned with, and she has already passed her ninety-first birthday. My father's sweet-natured younger sister, Gert, who must be eighty-six by now, is nevertheless still called the "kid sister."

Across the ocean in Israel, it is late spring in 2006. Yonah Steiner, fit and lean at eighty-one, bicycles across Kibbutz Ginosar to meet me for coffee at the Nof Ginosar snack bar on Shabbat. They say the past repeats itself. Here I am, like my grandfather Solomon before me, sitting with his brother Simon's son Yonah, at the same hotel table, even though twenty-six years have passed. We sit together, arm in arm, throughout the afternoon and talk about Steiner lives, about the family today, about Steiner family history, for hours and hours, until Rivkah sends out a search party to call us home for supper. Then we sheepishly creep back to the front porch of their little kibbutz cottage that looks out at the shimmering Kinneret to face Rivkah as she stands, veined legs bowed, arms akimbo, lips pursed in disapproval,

"*Yonah*," she reprimands in Hebrew, "Where have you been? Look at the time!" She shakes her head disapprovingly at me as if I'm the irresponsible party who led her charge astray.

Yonah bows his head and peeks up at her with guilty eyes compounded with boyish innocence, obedience, and love.

"*Eemah*," he says, and her heart melts then and there.

Rivkah pretends to be angry for a few more minutes, but she can't hold out. "*Nu*, the food is getting cold. Come to the table."

And the ritual of eating supper begins.

The Steiner genes are trademarked. You can spot them like a birthmark that jumps from generation to generation. My grandfather carried the Steiner mark on the crown of his head, heightened in intensity by a black satin yarmulke. Yonah bears the mark right on the inside crook of his arm. I wear the mark on my forehead, smack above my right eye. And when I lay out our family tree, the strongest Steiner lines of defense are easy to identify.

Today David Steiner, my grandfather's youngest son, rules our clan. My Uncle David doesn't wear a mark. Rather he puts his mark on everything he can. My father's younger brother is strong, smart, successful, stubborn; a brilliant businessman, an American Jewish/Israeli politico, a Democratic Party insider, a film-studio mogul (Steiner Studios), a real estate developer (Steiner Equities), a commissioner of the NY/NJ Port Authority, and a rainmaker who, in Bill Clinton's era, even slept in the White House in the Lincoln Bedroom (just with my Aunt Sylvia) and by Clinton's invitation, visited his namesake, Camp David. Inside the Steiner enclave, he tirelessly parades, orders, builds, presides, fund-raises, swaps jokes, performs, and, because deep down he is a softie where it really counts, takes care of us all — and there are many on this list.

In Israel, he supports branches of the family who are aging and ill. In America, beyond his own children and grandchildren, he helps his nieces and nephews and their children with college tuition and yearly rites of passage. He takes care of his brother and sisters, organizes bar mitzvahs and weddings, birthdays and funerals. To be absolutely accurate, the diplomatic dedication of my aunt Sylvia to the smooth sailing of all these affairs is critical to all my uncle's accomplishments. And we love her for it. However, it is Uncle David whom we call "The Godfather." And, in truth, he is.

When he asks you to do something, you just do it.

In 1999, my Uncle David asked me to do the impossible. The task: to persuade Yonah Steiner to return to Gromnik, Poland, on a Steiner family roots exploration trip.

"Tell him he can bring Rivkah. I'll cover all expenses for one week. I'm inviting all first-generation family. I'll charter a bus, a hotel, a plane — all arrangements will be taken care of. Just get him for me. This will be the trip of a lifetime!"

I had heard talk about this family trip all summer. Uncle David and Aunt Sylvia had conceived of a plan to return to the family roots and invited my grandfather's and grandmother's first-generation direct descendents to join them. The itinerary: Krakow, Tarnow, Tuchow, Gromnik, Rudnik-on-the-San, and Auschwitz.

My father, David's beloved, but Steiner-stubborn older brother, had already called in his RSVP.

"Nothing doing. Our parents left that place for a reason. Why would we go back? Not interested."

My father's vote did not deter his younger brother.

David called Israel twice to promote the plan. In Tel Aviv, the descendents from my grandmother's family were already pulling their suitcases down from behind the *boydems* (rooftop hot water heaters). The reception from my grandfather's side of the fence in Ginosar was less than enthusiastic.

"*Lo!*" Yonah flatly refused. "I won't go [back to Poland]! Let them all [the Poles] burn in hell!"

A month passes. The summer is almost over.

When the phone rings late one night while I'm in bed reading, I'm not surprised to hear Uncle David's voice on the phone.

"*Debish*, you know I'm trying to organize this family roots trip. Your father doesn't want to go — he's passing up a great opportunity," My uncle's voice pauses for a second and I wait him out, "but there will only be a trip if Yonah will join us. Without Yonah, there is no point. I've got a film crew and everything."

"So what do you need me to do?"

"Get Yonah to say yes. You're the only one who can speak to him. I'm counting on you to bring him on board. Just do it. Tell him I'll do anything he wants. *Please.*"

I know what needs to be done. Besides, I believe in the idea of this trip — a journey back to the home Yonah never returned to on that fateful day in 1939. Yonah is seventy-four years old when my uncle organizes this emotional powder keg of a trip. Now he hands me the fuse.

"Get back to me," my uncle says. "Tomorrow!"

I call Israel and first speak to my cousins, Yonah's sons. They are all in favor of the journey. Shimone and Amit want to go too. "But he'll never agree," Amit tells me. "And definitely not without my mother."

I hear Amit hem and haw, but even long distance I feel the hook catching his collar. "Okay, so try it. Talk to him. You never know. Maybe yes, maybe no. Who knows? If my mother says yes, and her doctor tells her she can make the trip, maybe he'll do it."

Yonah is holding all the cards, and I feel like a croupier who has been given a very long rake.

I dial again.

"No way!" Yonah shouts on the other end of the phone after hearing my point of view. Then a pause, another half-second of silence, and a small voice emerges, "And anyway, not without my wife! Not without *Rivkahle*!"

"Really?" I am surprised at how easily he capitulates.

Then another short silence in which I hear the wheels turning while Yonah continues his calculations, "I won't go without Rivkahle!" Another pause. "...*And* my sons! Tell *that* to David!"

Now I know he is hooked, but I am not clear on the terms.

"Yonah, I think it is first-generation only," I tell him. "I'm not even invited. I don't know about Shimone, Avi, and Amit."

"*Mah?!*" he trumpets as if he can't hear right. "What?! Wait just a minute! *Rega achad*!"

I listen as he readjusts his hearing aid, turning the earphone up to a screeching pitch which further agitates the static on the line. "What!?" he explodes. "*You're* not invited? Then *I'm* not going. *Period*!"

The next day I report the conversation to my uncle, word for word, in English.

Three days later, the tickets, itinerary and hotel information arrive in the mail. We are all going — twenty-one of us, including me, along with Yonah, Rivkah, Shimone, Amit, plus the Lichtstein/Shavit branch from Tel Aviv. Even my eighty-one-year-old Aunt Elsie hoists herself up on the bandwagon with a giant pocketbook I end up dragging through the salt mines of Wieliczka. Given one last chance to reconsider, my own father and his younger sister, Aunt Gert, politely decline.

"Dummies," Uncle David pronounces.

Suddenly the bus is full and we are off to Krakow, Poland, on the last week of September 1999, almost 60 years to the day since the German invasion of Poland.

CHAPTER EIGHTEEN: The Root Cellar

The farmhouse is still standing, guarding sixty years of another tenant's life history, from the time that war boots kicked down its front door on a September morning in 1939.

The house is an extended log cabin, Polish style, with a small, glassed-in side-entrance porch. It looks brown and dark, like a collapsed chocolate layer cake left under the pillow after a long-forgotten wedding night. Tired, poor, sagging at the jowls, the front of the brown cottage is brightened by simple white lace curtains that catch the autumn breeze from two tiny, half-opened, white-framed windows, whose peeling white-painted sills hold pots of ivy as old and neglected as the house itself. It is late September, early autumn in Poland, an Indian summer, quiet with the clearness of sky that comes after the leaves have turned red and orange; the sniff of burnt leaves tinges the air with the smell of harvest time and mingles with childhood memories of those first walks to school at the beginning of the new term.

Yonah, eyes intently focused on the narrow road, sits next to the bus driver the entire route from Krakow to Gromnik, pointing out familiar sites along the way: "*Heenay*! Here's the Schlanger's house! There – the bridge where the Germans grabbed me! *Ken, ken*...yes, the train tracks...Willi's finger. Go straight. There's the statue of the Virgin Mary! Turn here...*Lo*, no, not there...here!"

The bus driver turns right at the religious shrine and drives down a paved road lined with hundred-year-old oak and maple trees. "*Heenay*! Here!" he shouts in a stunned mix of English, Yiddish and

Hebrew. The bus driver pulls over to the side of the road, opens the bus door and Yonah, leading the way, strides down the road.

One by one, we all pile out onto the street pavement and look where Yonah is pointing. Off the main road, the Steiner holdings include a vast arm-sweep of tilled fertile farmland. The wide and meandering Biala River flows gently under the simple stone bridge on the right as we look toward Yonah's parents' house, with fields behind us running on for as far as the eye can see. "*Alles*, everything is my parents' land, your grandfather's land! *Alles Steiner*!"

Yonah enters the side gate of the farm compound, eyes as wide as a child's, taking in everything as if it were yesterday. There are several buildings nestled within the perimeters of the dilapidated chicken wire fence that surrounds the yard. His parents' original home still stands; my grandfather's sister Ciarna's house still stands. The ancient barn still stands, leaning against the decaying outhouse/privy, holding on to each another as if for dear life. Inside the small, dark, straw-strewn barn a milk cow chews, chickens strut, flies buzz. The well and its hand pump are coated with rust. The compound is muddy, dirty, unromantic, and does not have a Jewish feel at all.

In the center of the yard, squeezed between the original wooden outbuildings, stands a newly constructed stucco house, three floors high, with a proper wooden front door and an electric doorbell, a terracotta-tiled walkway, and a tangle of plastic pipes that looks as if they lead to running water and indoor plumbing.

But this is not the new house we are interested in.

Stepping through the metal garden gate into the inner yard, our translator and facilitator, Karin, introduces us to the present Polish resident of this farmhouse, who greets us quite shyly but with courtesy. Worn and aged, with straight gray-white hair held back behind her ears with a bobby pin, the old woman motions us to enter. The translator introduces the Steiner family to Anna Sterkowicz in English and Polish and Hebrew, and Anna listens intently to each and every one of our names. Then she steps forward, wipes her hands on her apron, and clasps Yonah's shoulder in shock and wonder, speaking at once to him in a gush of Polish, the words sputtering out as if she had been waiting for him for sixty years.

Yonah cocks his head, bending his good ear toward her, half in mistrust, half trying to recoup his understanding of Polish, until the translator assists with an explanation. Rivkah needs no help. Her Polish springs back to life as if it was a coil released from a rip in a threadbare sofa cushion. It is from Rivkah that I begin to understand who indeed is this Anna Sterkowicz and how she came to live on the Steiner property. As Anna speaks, Rivkah quickly translates the Polish into Hebrew directly into Yonah's almost deaf ear, but loudly enough for all of us to catch the tale.

She had been working in the fields behind Rachel and Simon Steiner's house that day in 1939, some sixty years ago, Anna explains, tears forming at the edges of her cloudy blue eyes. She was a peasant girl of eighteen, helping with the September harvest. She came to work for the Steiners daily from her neighboring village of Choinik. She saw it all. Of course she knew Yonah and his brothers. But Yonah was a little boy. She often helped inside the house with the laundry and the cleaning when she was not working in the fields. She knew his mother, Rachel, his father, Simon. She was especially close to Ciarna and her children. But after that morning in the fields, she never believed, never imagined she would see any of them, any Steiner, alive ever again.

She tells us how she watched from the fields, her body hidden low in the uncut wheat, as the German soldiers came to the house in a lorry nested with machine guns. She watched as the SS troops kicked open the door of Simon and Rachel's house, then Ciarna and Herschel's house, then old Grandmother Sarah's cottage in the back, and rounded up the family. She heard screaming, yelling, shouting. She watched as the soldiers shot the barking dog first, and then shot and killed Grandmother Sarah who had been screaming with terror that she was too old and too sick to move. The others, hands held high above their heads, were rounded up into the trucks and taken away. And suddenly, it was silent. The farm stood empty.

Anna pulls a handkerchief from her apron pocket and covers her toothless mouth as if it weren't too late to stop the truth from being told. Later, she says, she heard they took all the Jews from the village to the nearby town of Tuchow, where they were herded into the cobble-stoned square in front of the district Town Hall…and shot them all — women, children, men, the old, the young. Where the bodies were buried, she tells us, she has no idea.

That Yonah survived the war is a miracle.

Yonah listens, his face a mask. Skeptically, Rivkah looks on with one eyebrow raised.

Anna continues her story. She moved into the house with her husband after the war, she explains, when no one came back to claim it. A few years later, a Jew from Tarnow showed up with official-looking papers and sold them the property. Straightening her back with dignity, she adds quickly that her husband fought with the Soviets. And that he had died only a few years after his return from the army, leaving her a young widow with a small child. Today, her son, Bartok, lives with his wife and daughter in the new house they built on the grounds.

With a nod of her head, Anna Sterkowicz leads Yonah and the group from the chicken coop in the yard toward what was once Yonah's parents' house. We are led up the one concrete step through a bright, Polish-folk-blue-painted wood-framed doorway into the belly of the old house, crossing the threshold from present to past.

Yonah halts where the kitchen door is hanging off its hinges, shocked at the sight of the poverty and decay within. The small sliver of a linoleum floor sags with decades of neglect.

"Our kitchen was nothing like this," he says, confused by the ramshackle sight. "My mother would cook over there."

Yonah points to a stove that doesn't exist. His eyes search for the wood-burning stove with the beautiful blue tiles but instead find a jumble of ochre brown, factory-made ceramic squares running crookedly up the side of the wall between a tipped-over chimney stack and a rusty oven door.

"Our house was nothing like this," says Yonah in Hebrew, his voice low and disavowing. "*Lo kachah*. Not like this. My mother scrubbed the kitchen floor until it was shiny and slick enough to ice skate on! Our home was always in perfect order. My mother kept a clean kitchen, a kosher kitchen, with plates of home-cooked food always waiting for us on the table.

"My father built a strong house; a warm, welcoming house.

"A Jewish home."

Rivkah holds Yonah's arm and tries to quiet him, to remind him that he was a young child — that a child's memory enlarges over time. Yonah is having none of it. He shakes his head and sees his house through eyes that we do not possess. I stand behind him and look over his shoulder, trying to visualize every word he says. I can see his mother, Rachel, standing there by the soapstone sink, scrubbing the dirt from the turnips for the Sabbath soup, her black braid gathered down the length of her straight back, resting at the waist of a white linen apron with red embroidered flowers she had stitched herself. But the kitchen is left behind to its raw sweep of memory as we are quickly led deeper into the house.

A tour of the sleeping quarters follows. We walk through a small sitting area where one small window offers a peek out to the main road. A faded, fringed lace curtain shields a wilted potted ivy plant, abandoned on the white painted sill, from the autumn sun. A small wooden table set for one bridges the corner in the dim sunlight.

We move into a larger chamber whose plaster walls are washed a faded turquoise, and wood-beamed ceilings bend low to meet the stuccoed walls. The room is furnished with a wide wooden bed covered by a hand-crocheted coverlet, and an old-fashioned armoire is angled against the outer corner walls. The lumpy double bed, whose mattress sags in the center and is barely held up by a maple-colored matching wooden head-and-footboard, creates a stir of emotion.

Agitated, finger extended, Yonah argues with Rivkah in Yiddish and Hebrew, then swears with one hundred percent certainty that the double bed in the room belonged to his parents, dismissing with a hand wave the wooden crucifix that hangs on the wall above the pillow.

"*Nein, nyet*," Anna shakes her head, and Rivkah translates in Hebrew, "No, no, Yonah, this is not your parents' bed." Her words calm him down, but they do not convince him.

"*Abba, bo*!" Yonah and Rivkah's eldest son, Shimone, calls out to Yonah from the kitchen.

Nothing escapes Shimone when he is looking. And now he is looking for anything, anything at all that would speak to Yonah of his parents, his brothers, Willi, Rudi, and Paul — even a simple family photo, a scrap of newspaper, a tin box, or the true prize: the hidden cache of family treasures Yonah claims was stashed for safekeeping under the root-cellar stairs in the months before the war.

The trap door to the root cellar is a rough-cut outline barely visible in the marbelized pattern of the linoleum kitchen floor. Shimone pries it open with his strong kibbutz-worked hands. Proud of his discovery, Shimone points his father to the cellar stairs and the dark pit below.

"*Nu, Abba*, maybe something is still hidden behind one of the stairs?"

Yonah disappears below ground, deep into the darkness of the root cellar. It smells of cold, wet earth, root mold, a sour smell of decay as if the cellar hadn't been opened in half a century. From the kitchen trap-door opening, my uncle David tosses a pocket flashlight down to Yonah, who flashes the light around the bottom of the stairs pointing toward the belly of a cave-like cellar. The backlit stairs are hard to see, but as we descend behind Yonah, it is clear they are built of solid concrete; it's impossible to imagine access to a hiding place stuffed with a box of family treasures.

"These stairs are not the same," Yonah surveys the construction. "Our stairs ran down from the left side of the kitchen. They moved them."

"How do you know they're not the same stairs?" asks my uncle David who is a builder and knows about these things.

Yonah answers in a mix of Hebrew, Yiddish and English. "I remember because your grandfather and my father built the stairs together. I saw it with my own eyes. I stood at the top where the floor door opened and watched them."

There are eight of us crowded in this hole in the ground listening to Yonah as he stands, one elbow propped against the head-high, circular earthen wall, one hand motioning in the air, telling the story of how his mother would send him down into the cellar on Friday afternoons to collect the root turnips and parsnips for the chicken soup, or to bring up the potatoes that would roast with the chicken she was plucking for Shabbat dinner. How he could smell her cooking, he said, and almost taste it as if she were waiting for him right now upstairs in the kitchen, waiting for him to hurry with the vegetables. Yes, he could see her, her bright blue eyes smiling down at him, her strong hands giving him a push on his backside, her voice singing a shopping list in Yiddish. "Yonah, hurry, go fetch me a pail of potatoes and turnips before the sun sets and your father comes in from the fields." He was the youngest, Yonah explained, and therefore not yet in school. He was proud he could help her and didn't have to compete with his brothers for her attention. Friday afternoons were their special time together.

We stand, Amit, against the far wall, Shimone drops back into a shadow, his wife, Miriam, to the right of Yonah, the cameraman on the staircase, my uncle in the center of the cellar, and listen to my Shavit cousin, Gadi, as he translates Yonah's Hebrew into English.

"My mother," Yonah stutters, "*Myne mameh...*"

Sudden sobs of pain, anguish, longing and unexpressed grief wrack Yonah's body and he clings to the dirt walls and cries out, "*Eemaleh, Eemaleh, Eemaleh!*" calling for his mother over and over in plaintive, heart-wrenching cries like a lamb who has been yanked too early from the warmth of his mother's milk. Tears tumble out of Yonah's eyes, fresh wet tears, the size and appearance of fat swollen rain drops splashing down a window pane after a sudden cloud burst. Tears releasing seventy years of suppressed, blocked-up grief for which there was no solace — tears of sorrow and agony beyond normal comprehension.

I whisper to the cameraman and ask him to turn off his recorder. My uncle, my cousins, shift uncomfortably in their places, turning their faces away to afford Yonah the privacy of his pain. Miriam places her hand on Yonah's shoulder and looks into the air.

When the sobs slow and the tears ebb, Yonah fishes a handkerchief from his pocket and blows his nose. Slightly embarrassed, he raises his head and looks at us, then straightens up.

"*Zeh-oh,*" he says. "That's it. That's the way it was...And this is what is left."

He turns without another look behind him and walks back up the dark root-cellar stairs into the light.

CHAPTER NINETEEN: Finale

As the Hebrew version of the book, *Yonah al Chut Til,* was going to press for a Spring 2007 release by Yad Vashem, the Israeli Holocaust Museum, I spoke with Yonah by telephone from Boston to make certain he was still enthusiastic about the book — and to brace him for what was ahead. He spoke with his usual straightforwardness, and I listened to his clear Hebrew as if we were sitting in the same room chatting over a cup of coffee at Rivkah's kitchen table. Within two minutes, we were back in Poland again.

"It's been almost ten years," I say. "Tell me again what you thought when we went back. Are you glad you did it?"

Yonah's voice is strong and clear.

"You know the story. You were there with me, every step of the way. You didn't leave my side for one minute, so why do you have to ask me questions today about how I felt when we went back to Poland?"

But I know he wants to talk about it. "*Nu?*" I prod.

"Today, what do I remember? What do I think?"

"When I finally arrived at my family's home, it was very, very difficult. I went back in time seventy years. I can't explain my feelings. At that exact moment, I wasn't myself.

"I remember Rivkah told me to sit next to the bus driver and show him the way. And I did. When I saw the statue of the Virgin Mary by the train tracks, I knew that 200 meters further we turn right, cross the train tracks, and we'd arrive at the house. I knew the way, after all those years — everything came back to me like a boomerang. I don't know how to tell you what feelings I had at that exact moment. Seventy years of memories came back as if it was yesterday, and yet at the same time, I wasn't myself.

"To tell you the truth, up to the last minute, until I was outside my parents' house and saw it with my own eyes, I didn't believe that I had come home. I felt two conflicting emotions at work: one was a horrible, terrible feeling; the other was *simcha* — happiness. Even now, today, it is like a dream that passed in the night and is forgotten when you wake up in the morning.

"Dream or no dream, my memory of the road and the names of the people who lived here and there along the route was so present, it surprised Rivkah. She couldn't believe how a thirteen-year-old boy could remember names and places after all these years. But I saw the house right away from the bus. We stopped and got off, and Rivkah asked me where we could enter.

"I went up to the house and looked at this dilapidated structure and wondered how it could be so small, how the big, comfortable house of my childhood was in reality so small and so humble. I thought, *This can't be it*. I felt bad, very bad. I can't describe my feelings; I had such a bad, sinking feeling. I wasn't myself. I was in shock. Everything I remembered big was so small. Then I saw what was wrong — the front entrance that used to face the road had been moved to the side of the house. In its place, they had built a small porch.

"The rest of what happened inside the house you know. I don't need to talk about it again. But I want to tell you two things. A few years before our trip, Paul's daughter, Rachelle, took a trip from Paris and tried to visit our home and they wouldn't let her in. I don't know why. I don't know if they couldn't understand her, or they were afraid she wanted the property back, or what. She couldn't even set one foot inside the house. And here, your uncle David Steiner made it happen for all of us. He deserves a medal for opening the door.

I don't think a thing like this ever happened before, where one man takes his whole family back seventy years in time to their roots, to the place where his grandfather lived and his father was born; he returned me to my home that I had left at the age of thirteen. David is the only one who could make a thing like this happen.

"Today I am eighty-one years old. I never imagined that someone could want to do and do what he did. David deserves all the credit. It's a big thing. As I stood next to the house...I never believed I would ever set foot on that land again. And here I was, my eyes taking in the sweep of farmland my father owned and tilled, and I felt as though I was a shadow.

"You know, I didn't sleep before I went to Poland. My feelings were different from normal feelings. There's a difference between a grown man who leaves his home and family by choice and a child who is forced to disappear, against his will, and is gone for seventy years. You need a psychologist to explain this. And many nights in Poland I couldn't sleep. I existed in a different state altogether.

"It was seeing my parents' bed that shocked me the most, I can tell you. I swear that bed was my parents', one hundred percent. How am I certain? My brother Paul confirmed later when I described it to him by phone that it was the same bed — exactly the same wide bed with carved wooden head-and-footboard. And do you remember the room they wouldn't let us into? The room on the other side of the kitchen? That was where we boys slept. But the old lady said, *'No, you can't go in there, people are sleeping.'* We should have demanded to go in there. To see with our own eyes what was left from our family.

"I'm not sure — I could be wrong — but I don't think you can find anyone from Kibbutz Ginosar whose family history has evolved in the same way as this story. You have interviewed me and uncovered the facts, day by day, over the years, and you have written and put it together, and it's only special because who else would have come to interview me and pull out the words and piece the story together?

"This book is a journey that started when you were a girl of eighteen, and today, thirty-eight years have passed and you are still writing.

"Two things are unbelievable: Your will and courage to continue to write the book and then after that to push for the trip to Poland. And now you are still writing to update the story.

"And secondly, that there was a man who could make it happen. Your uncle, David Steiner, a man with power. I don't know people like this — such an important person — to have made the trip possible for all of us. I'm just saying the facts. 'Thank you' is not enough. I want to sign this 'thank you' with my birthright as a Steiner. You must tell him for me in English.

"It is a rare event, a once-in-a-lifetime occurrence, that you not only wrote the book and kept at it, but also that David is a man of strength and does what he says he is going to do. If he decides something...it's done. That's a Steiner trait. I'm also stubborn. I'm also difficult, but also I have a good heart. David is the same. Your grandfather, Solomon, the same. My father, my grandfather, all the Steiners, the same.

"I don't know how to explain my feelings toward you. I need to sit with a psychologist for days and weeks and months to understand this connection. Then, even the psychologist would go crazy waiting for me to explain myself. You and I think alike. Our feelings about things aren't far apart. Anyone listening to us speak would say we were brother and sister, or maybe twins. You are so like me. The way we think, our attitudes and private feelings, our natures are so similar. You are more than my daughter. I can't explain it, or find the right words, but you pushed me to open up, you kept at me, you dragged out this personal story in bits and pieces like shards of broken bones and joined them together again. There isn't anyone I know so young who could pull together a book like this, a story of five such concentrated years, who translated my scattered words into full sentences and has kept on going. I don't believe anyone else could have done it.

"Maybe I think that you are the only one who truly understands what being a Steiner means, what the name carries — the impulsiveness, the directness, the behavior, the drive — for the good, and for the bad. It's our nature. That's it; that's the way it is.

"There are not many who can understand the Steiners. We can be closed, remote, hard, short-fused, stubborn, difficult to live with, but if you take the time, you can discover our depth.

"Just ask Rivkah if I'm right. She'll tell you."

AFTERWORD

In late spring 2008, Yonah had a bad fall at work. The hospital in Poriya sent him home after a battery of heart tests and shrugged away anything serious, saying his arteries were as clear as new copper pipes and that his heart was as strong as a young man's. He had a hard fall, they explained, and he could expect his tail bone to hurt for while, only he needed to stay away from work. They gave him a shot of iron for good measure.

"I don't feel well," he complained after he was home for a week. "Something's not right. I can't eat."

After losing 10 kilos[24] in four weeks, he was back in the hospital for more tests, including a CAT scan and stomach and lung biopsies. The results were not good. Eventually Yonah was diagnosed with primary stomach cancer with an additional primary cancerous lesion on his lung. The prognosis was less than optimistic.

I found myself in Israel within the week sitting once again at Rivkah and Yonah's kitchen table, this time, however, surrounded by Yonah's sons, daughters-in-laws, and grandchildren. We Steiners took in the news as a family united in battle to save Yonah.

"Who do you call when you need a miracle?" I asked the table.

Everyone looked at me hopefully.

"Uncle David," I said, throwing out the one remaining ace from the last deck of cards in the pack.

The relief was palpable.

Within a day, the Steiners in America joined ranks. My uncle David told me he just happened to have invested in a new stomach-cancer-fighting drug that was in Phase I clinical trials at two New York hospitals. It seemed to have good results in shrinking metastasizing tumors. His surgeon son-in-law thought the drug would at least make Yonah more comfortable if Israeli doctors would agree to administer the infusions. There was a flurry of activity — phone calls back and forth to Israeli hospitals, arm-bending dinners with high ranking Israeli connections who could influence heads of oncology units in Israel to accept this trial drug, medical records faxed from Israel to New York and back, more phone calls, more emails — the campaign was inexorable.

Eventually chemotherapy was ruled out as being too late to help. And the miracle drug remained in New York.

"Leave him alone," Yonah's doctors advised. "We'll make sure he feels as comfortable as possible."

"How much time does he have?" The question no one wanted to ask was finally asked.

"We cannot predict what will happen with a person like this," came the response. "He's a survivor."

But the doctors could not look us straight in the eyes.

Today, almost one year later, I make another phone call from Boston to Israel after a long winter of worry, and my cousin Shimone answers. When I tell him that, by the way, I'm updating the last chapter of the book for the English edition and ask what I should write, he answers, "Write whatever you want, *just make sure there is no ending.*"

And here I leave you. Without an end. With hope for the future that good will prevail over evil. That the family will stay intact — even though I can already see the writing on the wall for the generation that led the way.

To Yonah. To Rivkah. To their bravery and heroism.

We Steiners that follow have a lot to live up to.

Author's Note: On May 26, 2009, one year after his diagnosis, and five days after we all came together in Israel to celebrate his 83rd birthday, Yonah Steiner passed away surrounded by his family and his beloved wife, Rivkah, at home in his bed on Kibbutz Ginosar. It should be written that in his epic battle with stomach, lung, and bone cancer, Yonah Steiner fought like a lion against the diagnosis, against the pain, against the morphine – until his very last breath.

APPENDIX

Letter from Kibbutz Ginosar Secretariat

Yonah Steiner's contributions to Kibbutz Ginosar

Yonah reached Palestine in January 1947, and went directly to Kibbutz Ein Gev, where his wife, Rivkah, was waiting for him.

The day after his arrival, Yonah, like a veteran kibbutz member, was assigned to work in the kibbutz and from the first moment his contributions were obvious and well-received.

After his first year in Ein Gev, and particularly after November 29, 1947, Yonah devoted himself to the war effort and began assisting in the production of landmines. He joined a sapper unit that laid landmines around the kibbutz boundaries — the mines that stopped the Syrian armored forces from breaking through the border during the War of Independence in 1948.

At the same time, Yonah participated in the production of two Davidkas [a homemade Israeli mortar], one of which was used in defending Ein Gev, and the other was sent to defend Safed, later becoming the monument that stands today in the center square of the city. Another of Yonah's unique activities was the welding of steel plates designed to protect the kibbutz trucks and the driver's cab. Armoring the driver's

cab made it possible to continue the kibbutz trans-
portation despite the danger lurking on the roads. At
a later stage, the road from Ein Gev to the Jordan
Valley was blocked, and on Yonah's orders a team from
the metal workshop dismantled the trucks, loaded
their parts on barges, and transferred them to
Tiberias. In Tiberias the trucks were reassembled and
they continued to serve Ein Gev while circumventing
the Arab roadblocks on the way to the Jordan Valley.

After Israel's Declaration of Independence and the
invasion of the Arab armies, a shipment of arms arrived
from Czechoslovakia, which comprised machine guns
whose operation instructions were in German. Yonah
was conversant in German and joined the team of
machine gunners. Later he was transferred to the
weapons center in order to service the arms.

When the war ended, Yonah joined the kibbutz drivers'
pool and in the following years drove trucks the
length and breadth of Israel.

In the early 50s, the Kibbutz Ha'meuchad movement
underwent an ideological and political split. Yonah,
Rivkah, and their eldest son, Shimone, moved to Kibbutz Ginosar, where Yonah was put in charge of one
of the branches of the metalwork shop in which he is
involved to this day. Several years later, he was put
in charge of the garage and thus became responsible
for the machinery, water irrigation, agricultural machinery, motor and tractor vehicles, and fields.

When he became the economic coordinator at Ginosar,
the kibbutz was in a period of development, and
Yonah was the leading figure. Both the water systems

and the machinery and tractor branches were outdated and inefficient, and it was imperative to adopt modern methods. This change involved great financial cost and the chances of raising capital were slim. However, Yonah harnessed himself to the issue, and undertook the task of seeking used and cheaper equipment. This idea aroused a great deal of opposition in the kibbutz. After all, the ongoing maintenance costs of used equipment would undoubtedly be extremely high, so claimed his opponents, and they warned that the system would collapse. But Yonah's standpoint was decisive. The equipment was purchased and financed by income from the field crops, and official approval was given. The regional water engineer, Emmanuel Tritesh, approved the request without hesitation, and when other kibbutzim approached him with a similar request, he refused, saying, "They have no Yonah Steiner; with him the system will work under even the most adverse conditions."

In 1965, after Wadi Zalamon dried up, the kibbutz was forced to dig a well in order to irrigate the citrus groves and install an appropriate pump. Once more Yonah rose to the occasion, and again Engineer Tritesh believed in his skills and abilities, and approved the project. Yonah had no training in installing wells, but the well worked properly for decades. Yonah also solved the problem of the lack of tractors to everyone's satisfaction. He purchased 20 used tractors at an extremely low price, and within a short time contributed to the upgrading of the agricultural branches of the kibbutz.

Rivkah and Yonah are the proud parents of three sons: Shimone, Avi and Amit, and the proud grandparents of five grandchildren. Yonah continues to work until this day. After hearing the story of his life and reading his book, I feel that 20th-century Jewish history will learn through stories like the story of Yonah's survival, and as we retell the story of the Exodus from Egypt, the next generations will retell these stories of the exodus of Jewish survivors from the Holocaust to Israel.

Uzi Velish

Secretary, Kibbutz Ginosar

2007

Yonah Steiner,
installing
irrigation pump,
Kibbutz Ginosar, 1965

Footnotes

[1] My grandfather was born Salamon Zelman Steiner in Poland and so named on the US immigration manifest; yet he wrote his name as Solomon Zelman (Z.) on all his US papers and that is how I knew him. Others called him "Sol" or "Saul," but Yonah knew him as Uncle Solomon.

[2] The word *yonah* in Hebrew means "dove," and is also the first name of the story's hero, Yonah Steiner. Hence the double meaning in the title of the book: "Dove (Yonah) on a Barbed Wire."

[3] In Polish, Tarnowa is pronounced "Tarnova"; I use the Polish spelling because that is the way the names appear in archives and documents.

[4] Yonah's father's name was written "Simche" on his Polish birth certificate, but his Polish name was Simon (Syzmon in Yiddish) and so it appears on documents. Yonah's eldest son, Shimone, is named after his grandfather's Polish name, Simon.

[5] Willi and Rudi's names on the birth records were Wolf (Zeev in Hebrew) and Rudolph/Jerucham. Poldek or Leopold's Jewish name was "Pesach."

[6] Pronounced "Charna."

[7] Bastards.

[8] About 1.25 miles.

[9] Pustkow is a small town in southeast Poland. In order to build the labor camp, the inhabitants of small villages were evacuated by force, and the villages burnt down. The first prisoners arrived at the camp in

1939; the majority were Jews from all regions of Poland. Due to the ruthless conditions, the majority of prisoners died or were executed in their first months in the camp.

[10] A little over six miles.

[11] About 124 miles.

[12] About 12.5 miles.

[13] Tarnow is a city in the south of Poland, east of Krakow, occupied by the Germans on September 8, 1939. The Nazis burned most of its synagogues the next day. On June 11, 1942, 13,500 Jews were deported to the Belzec death camp, and hundreds more were murdered in the city streets. On June 19, 1942, the ghetto was established. On September 10, all the ghetto's residents were ordered to report for selection, and about 8,000 were sent to Belzec. In October 1942 the Jews from the neighboring villages were sent to the Tarnow Ghetto, which was then liquidated on September 2, 1943 when some 7,000 Jews were deported to Auschwitz and the rest to the Plasow Ghetto slave labor camp outside of Krakow, the camp described in the book and movie, *Schindler's List*.

[14] About 300 feet.

[15] In the beginning, Mielec (pronounced "Mieletz") was a work camp and was later converted into a concentration camp; this is when identification marks (like Yonah's wrist mark "KL") were first tattooed on the arms of the Jewish prisoners in order to set them apart from the Polish forced laborers working in the camp.

[16] The shaved hairline down the center of the head was known by staff and prisoners as the "lice path." Yonah called it "the autostrada."

[17] A bit more than four lbs.

[18] Mauthausen (known from the summer of 1940 as Mauthausen-Gusen) grew to become a large group of Nazi concentration camps based on "extermination through labor" (*Vernichtung durch Arbeit*) that were built around the villages of Mauthausen and Gusen in Upper

Austria, roughly 20 kilometers (12.43 miles) east of the Austrian city of Linz.

The production output of Mauthausen-Gusen exceeded that of each of the five other large slave labor centers, including Auschwitz-Birkenau and Flossenburg in terms of both production quota and profits. Altogether, forty-five larger companies took part in making Mauthausen-Gusen one of the most profitable concentration camps of Nazi Germany.

[19] The rock quarry in Mauthausen was at the base of the infamous Stairs of Death. Prisoners were forced to carry rough-hewn blocks of stone — often weighing as much as 50 kilos (more than 100 pounds) — up 186 stairs. As a result, many exhausted prisoners in the front of the line, collapsed and fell on top of the other prisoners, creating a horrific falling domino effect all the way down the stairs.

[20] About 100 yards.

[21] Joint Distribution Committee, a Jewish organization that channeled funds to refugees during and after the war.

[22] There is some serious disagreement here over the facts. My Aunt Elsie (my grandfather's eldest daughter) claims that she herself sent a care package of socks and warm clothes from America to the kibbutz to help Yonah and his family. But my aunt remembers a discussion about whether or not the kibbutz had a share in the money and clothing received by their members as strict Socialist rules applied even to personal goods. My Aunt Elsie said that money, a dress, some socks, and clothes were sent to my grandmother Rose's brother Moshe's family in Tel Aviv so that Rivkah could pick the gifts up without telling the kibbutz. However, even to this day, Yonah insists that he had no help from my grandfather. And as memories are selective, I cannot attest to the actual facts. All I have proof of is an old envelope with Yonah's return address postmarked from Israel to my grandfather in 1951 and my 91-year-old Aunt Elsie's own memories of the events.

[23] Kibbutz Ein Gev sat on the eastern shore of the Sea of Galilee,

directly in target range of the Syrians who controlled the Golan Heights above. There was no road around the Kinneret in 1947. The only way to Ein Gev was by boat from Kibbutz Degania on the south perimeter of the lake or from Tiberias. At the time, the city of Tiberias was still under the British Mandate and had a large Arab population who was opposed to the new influx of Jewish immigrants. As it was only a handful of a months before the outbreak of the War of Independence in 1948, traveling from one Jewish settlement to another was extremely dangerous.

[2] About 22 pounds.

STEINER FAMILY: Genealogical notes

My great-grandfather Aharon, the patriarch of the Steiner family in Austria/Poland, was the fourth son and last child of my great-great-grandfather, Nahum Steiner, the first Steiner for whom we have documentation. Born in Berlin, Germany, in 1820, Nachum apparently migrated eastward into the Austrian Empire and settled in the region referred to as Galicia.

As Nachum's other children dispersed, Aharon remained and took over the family farm. They say history repeats itself, and it is interesting to note that my grandfather Solomon was Aharon's fourth son and he too became the patriarch of our branch of the family. My uncle David Steiner, who is Solomon's fourth child and named after Solomon's younger brother David who was gassed as a soldier in WWI, took up the family baton as patriarch of the present generation of American Steiners, and that is where it remains today. In the Israeli branch of the Steiner family, the patriarchy of the family lies in the hands of Yonah Steiner, the hero of *Dove on a Barbed Wire*. Yonah, like his father, Simche, and his grandfather, Aharon, was also the fourth son.

One can also trace the evolution of the ancestors' names on the Steiner Family Tree as evidenced through the American, Israeli, and French derivations of Rachels, Sarahs, Jeruchams, Simches, Aharons, and so forth, in the contemporary generation of Steiners. Also to be noted is that the varied spellings of the ancestor names are not inconsistencies but accurate recordings of the archival information I have researched. Because so many of my cousins and their parents have been named after deceased family in Europe, I have used the original spellings as they appeared in birth certificates, true to their Polish or Jewish origins, in case anyone ever wishes to trace the family back in time utilizing the accurate genealogical information as presented in this tree.

For example, my grandfather Solomon's eldest son and my own father, who is listed as "Alfred N." on the family tree, was born in the USA and legally registered as Nachum Aharon Steiner on his birth certificate — named after his grandfather Aharon and great-grandfather Nachum. Because my father was the first American-born son of European immigrants, and like most first-generation children wanted to meld seamlessly into the American culture, he refused to answer to his foreign-sounding birth name even as a child. So he swapped his middle name with his first name and Anglicized it from Aharon to Alfred. (For my father, the name "Nachum" was completely unacceptable, hence the initial "N.")

Rachel became Rachèlle in France and Rose in the United States; Jerucham (Rucham) became Rudy in Poland, Rudi in France, and Jerry or Gerome in the United States. Sarah, the family matriarch from Zawada, Poland, became "Sue, Sura, Sandy," in America. Simche or Simon, Yonah Steiner's father, who perished in Poland, evolved into Steven, Stephen, or Scott in America, and Shimone in Israel.

Ciarna (Charna) and Chana (Annie) although close in spelling, are not the same names. Chana (Hannah/Annie) was Ciarna's older sister and it was she who used to sneak food to her younger sister when Ciarna (Charna) started seeing her future husband, the rascal Hersch Mannsdorf, and was locked out of the house back in Poland. Chana became Annie in the United States, leaving Ciarna behind in Europe to fend for herself.

As he was born in Israel, Yonah's eldest son, Shimone, was named after Yonah's father, Simche Steiner (as it is written on his birth certificate). Simche's name in Polish was Szymon. Simon in Hebrew is Shimone.

Lastly, my own name, Deborah Sarah (Sue) or, as my grandfather would call me, "Devorah Sura," was designated by my grandfather in memory of his brother Hershel's wife, Dacha Wildenstein, and his mother (my great-grandmother), Sarah Zorn Steiner, both of whom perished in the Holocaust.

Other family facts and lore about the Steiners of Europe have been included as footnotes in the text or as story boxes in the Family Tree. [See pullout insert at back of the book].

ACKNOWLEDGMENTS

I wish to thank the many, many people whose encouragement and support made this book possible:

AND TO ALL OF THOSE WHO READ THE BOOK IN HEBREW AND DEMANDED AN ENGLISH TRANSLATION.

My uncle David Steiner and my aunt Sylvia Steiner, who protected me, encouraged me and stood firmly behind me for as long as I can remember. They have led the way for all the Steiners, with generosity of spirit, strength of purpose, and loving hearts.

My grandfather Solomon Steiner (z"l), whose throaty laugh, strength, and strong will — and tomato plants — I sorely miss, and to whom I have dedicated the Steiner Family Tree.

My grandmother Rose, who was so brave at such a young age, and who had the courage to take the train ticket from Rudnik in place of her sick sister and traveled so far to make a new life in America.

My father, Alfred Steiner, who provided the substance and the heart.

My aunt Elsie Selikoff, who is the true family historian with a most incredible memory — and shared it all with me.

My aunt Gert McConville Nudel, for her e-mails and caring.

My Steiner relations in the U.S.A.: cousins, Ellen, Nancy, Doug, and Jane; Judy, Mark, Ronnie, Steven, and Gary; my sisters, Joan and Barbara, and my daughter, Kierie Steiner van Rooyen, who are continuing our family line with strength, courage, and determination – you all carry the Steiner mark. Never forget your roots.

THE STEINERS OF GINOSAR:

First and foremost, Yonah and Rivkah Steiner, who are and will always remain close to my heart and who, with great patience, edit after edit, phone call after phone call, visit after visit, both gave me so much.

Shimone, Avi, and Amit Steiner, Yonah and Rivkah's three sons and my cousins, who became my brothers for life.

Liora Steiner and Miriam Ron, *HaKallot*, for being there when I couldn't.

The Steiner grandchildren, Benjamin; Gabi and Adi; Shai and Eden — so you may always remember the heroic story of your grandparents.

LICHTSTEIN RELATIVES IN TEL AVIV/HERZLIYA:

Adi Shavit, who was the original *shaliach* when he convinced me to make Israel my first stop on my secret passage to Japan in 1969. The real journey started then.

Navah Shavit, who welcomed me and gave me her couch to park on for the rest of my life.

Gadi, Tamar, and Ami Shavit, who are my special "children."

Great Uncle Baruch Moshe and Elke Lichtstein (z"l), my grandmother Rose's gentle brother and his wife in Tel Aviv, who gave me their hearts and home when I was a young girl.

Shlomo and Vicky Ben-Dor/Lichtstein: Vicky, a brave Etzel underground fighter, who also has a remarkable story to tell, and to another silent warrior, Shlomo, who keeps going despite the obstacles.

David, Bathsheva, Little Shlomo, and all the Lichtstein cousins, who welcomed me without reservation into their lives in the early days of my aliyah.

THE STEINERS OF PARIS, FRANCE:

Leopold (Poldek) Steiner (z"l), who sadly wasn't on the "Return Journey" with us, and whose silver tailor's sewing thimble and threaded needle I keep as a fond remembrance.

Rachelle Steiner, Paul's devoted daughter of the Steiner's French branch who was the first to start the search for her grandparents, Rachel and Simon.

Collette Steiner, wife, mother, and historical witness, who kept the facts straight.

Rudi, Cyril, Matteo, and Alexis-Leopold Steiner, who are perpetuating the Steiner name in France for generations to come.

THANKS, AS WELL, TO:

The staff of Simcha Publishing Company: Yaacov Peterseil, who read the English manuscript in "one gulp" and accepted it for publication; **Daniella Barak**, who guided these pages through all the stages of production; **Dvora Kiel**, whose brilliant editorial light shone through from the other end of the long book-creating tunnel.

Carolyn Hessel of the Jewish Book Council, who connected this book to a worldwide audience and gave me incredible support from the very first step.

The staff at Yad Vashem: Shaya ben Yehuda, Bella Gutterman, Miriam Talisman, Mark Shraberman, who helped me unstintingly with the publication of the original manuscript in Hebrew; and Yaacov (Jacob) Rosen, who pointed me toward the Yad Vashem archives to begin with.

My treasured friends at Kibbutz Ginosar: Inger Ronen, who was there with me from the beginning and snapped that irreplaceable photograph of Yonah and me in her kitchen the last night before she packed up to return to Sweden; **Rut Allon**, who started me on this extended project twenty-eight years ago in her belief that Yonah's story needed to be told both in English and Hebrew; **Uzi and Connie Velish**, who recognized Yonah's and Rivkah's remarkable achievements and lasting contribution to the kibbutz; and all the *chaverim* of Kibbutz Ginosar who recognized a hero amongst them.

POLAND

I cannot conclude without thanking the following people who assisted me with research and support in Poland in 2006: Klezmer-Hois; Wojtek Ornat and staff; Leopold Kozlowski; Chris Schwarz (z"l), Director of the Galicia

Jewish Heritage Museum; Andrzej Nadurski, driver; Ewa Bialkowska, principal, Gromnik Grammar School; Ursula Marszalek, Gromnik Grammar School English class teacher; Kerota and Helena Sterkowijcz and grandmother Anna Sterkowjcz (Gromnik); Jan Chamura, researcher at Tarnow Archiwum; Authorities at Tuchow Town Hall and Tarnow Town Hall.

UNITED STATES

Thank you to St. Regis College's Spellman Museum of Postal Stamps in Weston, Massachusetts, and to the archival research efforts of curator, **George Norton.**

Special thanks to: Ami and Efrat Shavit, for creative consulting, editing, and for finding just the right title for the book; **Tamar Shavit and Shimone Rothstein**, for the remarkable family portraits; and **Gad Shavit**, for taking on overwhelming responsibility as the Hebrew/English translator on our family-roots trip to Poland.

Lastly, this English version would not have been possible without the volunteer editorial support of my old and trusted friend, **Dory Warner Greene.**

About the Author

After leaving the United States for Israel in 1969 to work as a volunteer on Kibbutz Ginosar, Deborah Steiner-van Rooyen completed her university education in Jerusalem at The Hebrew University. In 1973, she joined the army settlement of Nachal Yam in the Sinai, and then traveled extensively through Southeast Asia and Japan, where she worked as a freelance photographer. Her later adventures have taken her to South Africa and Egypt, and in the mid-1990s to Amman, Jordan, where she worked as a design consultant for The Noor al Hussein and The Jordan River Foundations helping the women of rural villages and Palestinian refugee camps develop nature-oriented crafts, rugs, jewelry, and textiles for export markets (www.jordanriver.jo), (www.nooralhusseinfoundation.org).

Currently, Deborah works as an international investigations specialist/private investigator specializing in the location and recovery of missing persons and parentally-abducted children (www.acertainjustice.com), as well as researching and assisting in the reunification of families dislocated by war or natural disasters. She is also the creative director and owner of a graphic design and communications studio (www.dvrdesign.com) in Boston.

In 2002, Harper Collins published her last memoir: *Boat Bastard, a Love/Hate Story*. Her daughter, Kierie van Rooyen, a former student at Tel Aviv University, is now studying veterinary medicine abroad.

Deborah remains in close contact with her family on Kibbutz Ginosar and in Tel Aviv and returns to Israel frequently. For more information and author updates, please visit www.DoveonaBarbedWire.com.

FAMILY
PHOTO ALBUM

In the beginning. Author's great-grandmother, Sarah Zorn Steiner, and great-grandfather, Aharon Steiner, in front of farmhouse in Gromnik, Poland. (*Photo taken by author's grandfather, Solomon Steiner, during his last and final trip to Poland from the USA to visit his parents on Passover, 1932*).

Simche (*father of Yonah*) Steiner's birth certificate as recorded in 1887 in Olszowa, Galicia.

8	9 Eigenhändige Unterschrift, Beschäftigung und Wohnort Własnoręczny podpis, zatrudnienie i miejsce zamieszkania		10	11	12
nb Zuname der Mutter, Stand und Wohnort, n Bor- und Zuname, öftigung und Wohnort ihrer Eltern	der Pathen oder Zeugen, des Sandels oder Schemes *kumów lub świadków, Sandeka lub Schames'a	des oder der Beschneidenden obrzezującego lub obrzezujących	Der Hebamme oder des Geburtshelfers akuszera lub akuszerki	Todt geborene Kinder Dzieci nieżywo urodzone	Anmerkung U w a g a
ie i nazwisko, stan, ce zamieszkania matki i jej rodziców					
Sara corske iórcha i radt Corn spinatoric x Zawadne h. wayszez	Nuchym Steiner fynsam " Olerony	Lewi Grober fynsan w Zorn	Wikdorys Nojtowske wyrobnica w Olsary		Przyznaję się do ojcowstwa w obec świad Rów No 81 Aron Steiner

(Transl.) **Birth Certificate – Simche Steiner (Yonah's father):** Born third day of November 1887; Place of Birth: Olszowa; House Number: 19; Day of Circumcision or Conferral of Name: November 10, 1887, in Olszowa. Child's first name: Simche; Sex: Male; Legal Status: Illegitimate*; Father: Aharon Steiner, innkeeper in Olszowa. Mother and her parents: Sarah (Sura), daughter of Peisach and Fraidl Zorn, innkeepers in Zawada, Nowy Sącz District; Godfather: Nachum Steiner, innkeeper in Olszowa; Circumciser: Lejser Grober, innkeeper in [illegible]; Midwife: Wiktoria Wojtowska, irregular occupation in Olszowa; Remarks: Father Aharon Steiner confessed to his paternity in the presence of the witnesses. *Jewish children were illegitimate status from the point of view of the authorities as rabbinical marriages were not registered with the local authorities.*

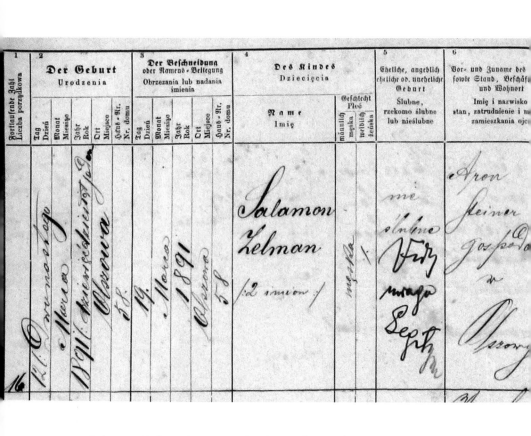

Solomon (*Salamon*) Steiner's birth certificate of author's grandfather as recorded in 1891 in Olszowa, Galicia .

(*Below Transl.*) **Birth Certificate – Salamon Zelman Steiner (Simche's younger brother and author's grandfather):** Born Twelfth of March 1891; Place of Birth: Olszowa; House Number 58; Day of Circumcision or Conferral of Name: March 19, 1891 in Olszowa. Child's First Name: Salamon Zelman; Sex: Male; Legal Status: Illegitimate*; Father: Aharon Steiner, farmer in Olszowa. Mother and her parents: Sarah (Sura), daughter of Peisach and Fraidl Zorn, innkeepers and landowners in Zawada, Nowy Sącz District; Godfather: S. [illegible] Topfgang, farmers in Palesnica; Circumciser: Lejser Grober, innkeeper in [illegible]; Midwife: Maryanna Logeza, in Palesnica; Remarks: Father Aharon Steiner confessed to his paternity in the presence of the witnesses. *Jewish children were illegitimate status from the point of view of the authorities as rabbinical marriages were not registered with the local authorities.*

	8	9 Eigenhändige Unterschrift, Beschäftigung und Wohnort Własnoręczny podpis, zatrudnienie i miejsce zamieszkania		10	11	12
b Zuname der Mutter, Stand und Wohnort, r Vor- und Zuname, ftigung und Wohnort ihrer Eltern · i nazwisko, stan, e zamieszkania matki i jej rodziców	der Pathen oder Zeugen, des Sandeks oder Schemes kumów lub świadków, Sandeka lub Schames'a	des oder der Beschneidenden obrzezującego lub obrzezujących	Der Hebamme oder des Geburtshelfers akuszera lub akuszerki		Todt geborene Kinder Dzieci nieżywo urodzone	Anmerkung Uwaga

Required by the regulations of the Secretary of Commerce and Labor of the

S. S. _Grosser Kurfürst_ _____ sailing from

2		3	4	5	6	7	8
NAME IN FULL		**Age.**	**Sex.**	**Married or Single**	**Calling or Occupation.**	**Able to—**	**Nationality.** (Country of which citizen or subject.)
Family Name.	Given Name.	Yrs.	Mos.				Read.	Write.	
Köster	Erna	17			nurse	yes	yes	Germany
Speiser	Thiel	23		m	s	diamond grinder			Austria
Kürg	Haidar	86		m	s	tailor			"
Steiner	Salomon	20		m	s	tailor			"

SS _Grosser Kurfürsh_ Manifest List of Alien Passengers for the United States sailing from Bremen, Germany, on November 21, 1912. Solomon Steiner (originally spelled "Salomon") is listed as passenger #4, age twenty years, single male, from Gromnik, Galicia, son of Aharon Steiner. Destination: Freeland.

Tarvan	Lucef	25		m	s	theologe			Austria
Gärtner	Leiser	23		m	s	tailor			Croatia
Böhm	Theresia	37		f	m	housewife			Hungary
Medisoch	Hermine	18		f	s	maid			"
Gymana	Josef	45		m	m	merchant			"
Tajder	Otto	30		m	m	merchant			Germany
— " —	Clara	19		f	m	housewife			"
Everding	Mina	28		f	m	housewife			"
Troegel	Rosa	38		f	m				"
— " —	Adolf	10		m	s	student			"
Lehmann	Bertha	32		f	s	dressmaker			"
Fischer	Rosa	26		f	s	childrens nurse			"
Mannsberg	Erich	20		m	s	technologist			"

tates, under Act of Congress approved February 20, 1907, to be delivered

_Bremen_____, _November_, _2ᵗʰ_, _1912_

	10		11	12	
	*Last Permanent Residence.		The name and complete address of nearest relative or friend in country whence alien came.	Final Destination. *(Intended future permanent residence.)	
	Country.	City or Town.		State.	City or Town.
	Germany	_Friedenruck_	_brother: Henry Klein_ _Mifterга Hungary 53 Friedenruck_	NY	_New York_
	Galicia	_Rzeszow_	_father: Leib Spinner_ _Rzeszow, Galicia_	"	"
	NON IMMIGRANT ALIEN	_N.Y. New York_	_mother: Cheje Hirsz_ _Tarnow, Galicia_		
	Galicia	_Gromnik_	_father: Chaim Heiss_ _Gromnik, Galicia_	"	_Freeland_
	"	_Stry Zmigrod_	_wife: Henny Weinstein_ _Holy Zmigrod, Galicia_	"	_Brooklyn_
	Switzerland	_Metzindorf_	_mother: Mathe Schammel_ _Blагraze 19, Biel_	Ill	_Elgin_
	"	_Deitigen_	_wife: Rosa Spöttes_ _Ottingen, Ct. Solothurn_	"	"
	Bohemia	_Schönfeld_	_brother: Anton Loslan_ _Schönfeld i/ Bohemia_	NY	_New York_
	Galicia	_Rzeszow_	_father: Salomon Grünes_ _Rzeszow, Galicia_	"	"
	Hungary	_Felsöläre_	_mother: Karl Palotes_ _Michelgasse 39, Wien XVI_	Ill	_Chicago_
	"	"	_parents: Dоry Medipes_ _Okersehinger, Hungary_	"	"
	"	_Telовrismyö_	_wife: Maria Euгаria_ _Velovrismyö, Hungary_	NY	_Saratoga Sp._
	Germany	_Schmalkalden_	_father: Max Spinoles_ _Klingen i/ Thüringen_	"	_Brooklyn_
	"	"	_father ill_	"	"
	NON IMMIGRANT ALIEN	_N.Y. Fort Wayne_	_father: Heinr. Windtreat_ _Volksschule i/ Harnzow_	Ind.	_Fort Wayne_
	NON IMMIGRANT ALIEN	_Wisc Milwaukee_	_father: Heinrich Strange_ _Rheinmühlenstr 39, Midland Park_	Wisc	_Milwaukee_
	NON IMMIGRANT ALIEN		_grandfather:_	"	"
	Mrs. Anna Brown		_sister: Mrs. Wehle_ _Reichstr. 18, Dresden_	Mass	_Boston_
	NON IMMIGRANT, ALIEN		_father: Josef Fischer_ _Wellhausen i/ Bavaria_		
	Germany	_Leipzig_	_father: Ch. Mannborg_ _Friedehstr. 18, Leipzig_	NY	_New York_

(*Right*) **Solomon Steiner on his wedding day on March 25, 1917 in Trenton, New Jersey** to 18-year-old Rose (*Rachel*) Lichtstein, daughter of Eli Melech Lichtstein and Shandel Waschlicht of Rudnik nad Sanen. Rose emigrated to the USA at age 16 and worked as a couture seamstress in Trenton, NJ, 1915. She beaded the inaugural gown worn by President Warren Harding's wife.

Solomon and Rose Steiner's house on 231 Pomona Avenue in Newark, NJ, 1925. Solomon bought the corner lot, once a piece of Lyon's Farm, designed and built this house in a developing neighborhood located in the Weequahic district of Newark that soon became home to many Jewish immigrants from Europe who prospered in America. (Author Philip Roth wrote about Jewish life in this enclave in books *Portnoy's Complaint* and *Goodbye Columbus*). During the Depression years, Solomon worked three jobs to take care of his four children and wife along with various European relatives who lived with them as they got a foothold in the new country, while still managing to send money home to Poland. Eventually he reconfigured the house into four flats. After WWII, Solomon's youngest brother, Sidney, opened a kosher catering reception hall called "Steiner's Caterers," which became the gathering place for all family events until the early 1950s when the community moved out of Newark to the suburbs.

Family Portrait (*L-R*) Gertrude, Elsie, David, Solomon, Rose, and Alfred Steiner (*author's father*) March, 1932.

Rok szkolny 19 _38_ / _39_

1	Nr p. Nazwisko i imię ucznia		12 Steiner Jonas
2	Imię ojca i matki		Szymon Rachela
3	Data (dzień, miesiąc i rok) i miejsce (miejscowość i powiat) urodzenia		15 maj 1926 r. Gromnik pow. Tarnów
4	Wyznanie		mojżesz.
5	W którym roku szkolnym wstąpił do szkoły i do której klasy		1932/33 pierwszy
6	Nazwa szkoły i klasy do której uczeń uczęszczał przed wstąpieniem do tej szkoły		
7	Który rok jest w danej klasie		pierwszy
8	**Oceny ustalone z końcem okresu**		I II III
9	z sprawowania		
10	z religii		
11	z języka polskiego		
12	z języka		
13	z historii		
14	z geografii		
15	z nauki o przyrodzie		
16	z arytmetyki z geometrią		
17	z rysunku		
18	z zajęć praktycznych		
19	ze śpiewu		
20	z ćwiczeń cielesnych		
21	z		
22	Liczba dni opuszczonych	w okresie	I II III w całym roku szkolnym
		ogółem	12 10 6 28
23		nieusprawiedliwionych	— — — —
24	Liczba spóźnień		— 1 — 1
25	Orzeczenie Rady Pedagogicznej w końcu roku szkolnego i w razie niepromowania jego uzasadnienie		
26	Data wydania duplikatu		
27	Motywy ocen niedostatecznych i uwagi		

SZKOŁA PODSTAWOWA
im. Wincentego Witosa
33–180 Gromnik, ul. W. Witosa 4
tel./fax (0–14) 651–42–29
000718588

Za zgodność z oryginałem

GROMNIK, dnia 11. 10. 2006 v.

p.o. DYREKTOR SZKOŁY

mgr Ewa Białkowska

In 2006, the author returned to Gromnik to search for Steiner birth certificates and property deeds. Told by the Gromnik town clerk that all local Jewish birth certificates were destroyed in WWII, the author did not give up. Determined to find a record of Yonah's existence, she walked into the Gromnik Grammar School and convinced the school prinicipal to search the school's archives for any records of Yonah's or his brothers' school attendance. The school principal, Ewa Bialkowska, spent the evening searching through the archives in a warehouse basement, and came up with the actual school report card of Yonah's last year repeating the 6th grade in 1939. The Polish teacher's notations are confirmation of Yonah's birth date, May 15, 1926, and an acknowledgment that he was registered as the son of Szymon and Rachel Steiner of Gromnik. This report card record, stamped and certified, is now his official birth certificate.

Also note: Yonah got very low marks on his "behavior" and was often absent from class, which caused him to repeat the 6th grade, a class he was never able to complete. His fate, instead, was to fall into the hands of the German SS on his walk home from school in September 1939, and he "graduated" six years later from a series of German slave labor and concentration camps.

(*Above*) **Yonah's last school record, 1938/1939,** recovered by author from Gromnik Grammar School archives in 2006.

The original Gromnik Grammar School building serves as the Gromnik Town Hall and municipal health offices today. Births of local Jewish children were not included in the town register and were kept in the local synagogue. All records of Jewish life were subsequently burned or destroyed during the Nazi Occupation. *

(*Right*) **The bridge over the Biala River** in Gromnik Center where the SS grabbed Yonah on the way home from school in 1939.

(*Left*) **The path home.** Yonah's walk home from the Gromnik Grammar School led through this arborway to the main street of the village.

*No known childhood photos of Yonah, his brothers, or his parents survived the war. (*Despite searches through boxes of photos discovered in America, the author could not locate photographs of any of the European Steiners other than the picture portrait of Aharon and Sarah Steiner at the Gromnik farmhouse taken by Solomon Steiner on his last visit to Poland in 1932.*)

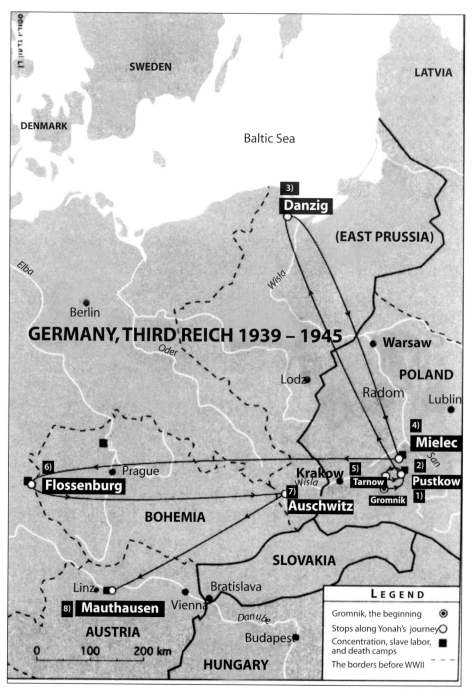

Map of Yonah Steiner's six-year journey of survival from his home village of Gromnik, Poland, in September 1939, to liberation from Mauthausen Concentration Camp in Linz, Austria, on May 5, 1945. The route traces Yonah's path from Gromnik to: 1) **Pustkow** (from first escape and return to second imprisonment); 2) **Pustkow**; 3) **Danzig** (*Gdansk*) in an East Prussian submarine factory; 4) **The Tarnow Ghetto**; 5) **Mielec**; 6) **Flossenburg**; 7) **Auschwitz**; and 8) **Mauthausen**.

Last Stop: Mauthausen Concentration Camp (*Gusen*). Yonah's Prisoner Card dated 10/1944. Liberation came to Mauthausen seven months later on May 5, 1945.

Camp survivor friends (*L*) and Yonah Steiner (*R*), Germany, 1945.

(*Above*) **Yonah Steiner, Rome, Italy, 1945,** wearing his first tailored clothes earned in return for working for an Italian sheet metal fabricator. The job lasted one week.

Posing in uniform with American soldiers under a Roman fountain, 1945. Yonah (*far right*) worked for the postwar American forces in Italy as a lorry driver.

Yonah Steiner, 1945.

Yonah Steiner, 1946.

Yonah Steiner, 1946 – 47 Training with the Haganah School for Seamanship in Hamburg, Germany.

Rivkah (Regina) Zinger, dressed in Polish Partisan uniform borrowed from a friend for this portrait. Blanke-nessen, Germany, 1946.

(L-R) **Survivor friends.** Frieda Charny, Yonah Steiner, and Rivkah Zinger, Blankenessen, Germany, 1946.

Blankenessen, Hamburg, Children's House, 1946

Childrens' House, Blankenessen, Hamburg, Germany, 1946, set up by the Joint Distribution Committee to aid orphaned Jewish refugees and dislocated families, is where Yonah and Rivkah met. They were married within two weeks.

Paul Steiner escorting Yonah's new wife, Rivkah Zinger Steiner, to Marseille to board ship for legal passage to Palestine, 1946.

Paul Steiner's business card from his atelier in Paris, France, where he settled after the war with his French wife, Collette LeFèvre Steiner.

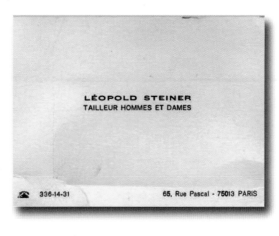

LÉOPOLD STEINER
TAILLEUR HOMMES ET DAMES

☎ 336-14-31   65, Rue Pascal · 75013 PARIS

Yonah and Rivkah Steiner crossing the Kinneret (The Sea of Galilee) on the boat "Akiva" to Kibbutz Ein Gev, 1947. Rivkah is pregnant with her soon to be firstborn son, Shimone.

Yonah Steiner testing new machine gun assembled in Kibbutz Ein Gev, 1947, shortly before the outbreak of the War of Independence.

Yonah and Rivkah's three sons: (*Above*) Shimone Steiner and (*below* L-R) his brothers, Amit and Avi Steiner, Kibbutz Ginosar, 1969.

(*Above*) **Kibbutz Ginosar, 1969.** Yonah Steiner (age 43) and author, Deborah Steiner (age 18), near the Volunteers' Quarters in Ginosar.

(*Right*) **The author's Israeli identity card,** issued in September 1969.

(*Below*) **Author (age 22) at Nachal Yam,** an army-based fishing settlement in Sinai, 1973, just before the outbreak of the Yom Kippur War.

(*Above*) **Kibbutz Ginosar, 1973.** Author's grandparents, Solomon Steiner and Rose Lichtstein Steiner, visiting Yonah and family after making Aliyah to Israel.

(*Above Right*) Solomon Steiner sits with nephew Yonah's sons Amit (*L*) and Avi Steiner (*R*), Kibbutz Ginosar, 1973.

(*Above*) Author's grandparents and Yonah Steiner touring Israel, 1973.

(*Above*) **Paul Steiner**, Orleans, France, 1998.

THE RETURN, 1999

(*Above*) **Rivkah Steiner,** Krakow, Poland, 1999.

Yonah's reaction as the bus approaches his home in Gromnik, Poland. Cousin Gad Shavit sits next to him (*R*).

Yonah's parents' home, still standing in Gromnik, Poland, 1999.

(*Above*) **Yonah points to the family fields** and extent of Steiner property. (*Below*) Yonah's hand on his cousin David's shoulder as he tours the farm.

(*Above*) **The Biala River** bordering the Steiner property, Gromnik, Poland, where Yonah and his brothers played as boys.

(*Above*) **Anna Sterkowicz, 1999**. Anna's family took over the empty Steiner farm and moved into Yonah's parents' house after WWII.

(*Above*) **Yonah and Rivkah listen to Anna** tell of how she worked for Yonah's parents before the war and how she saw his parents rounded up by the SS while she was hiding in the wheat fields behind the house.

(*Above*) **The kitchen**. What was once Yonah's mother's spotless kitchen lies in disarray.

(*Above*) **Yonah's parents' bed still remains.** The chimney and wood-burning stove, (*left*) however, are no longer tiled with blue and white artisan's tiles.

The Root Cellar. The cellar entrance is discovered by Yonah's son, Shimone Steiner, under a linoleum floorboard in the kitchen, 1999.

(Above) **David Steiner and his eldest daughter, Ellen Steiner Dolgin,** standing in the Tuchow town square where the Steiner family was shot by the Nazis SS.

(Above) **Author Deborah Steiner and Yonah Steiner,** Kibbutz Ginosar, 2004 (*photgraph courtesy of Inger Ronen*).

David Steiner takes us back to our family roots to Poland, September 1999. (*Below*) Visiting his parents' gravesite.

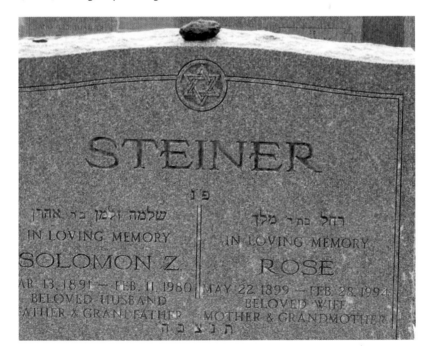

STEINER

פ נ

שלמה ולמן בר אהרן   רחל בתר מלך

IN LOVING MEMORY   IN LOVING MEMORY

SOLOMON Z.   ROSE

MAR. 13, 1891 — FEB. 11, 1980   MAY 22, 1899 — FEB. 28, 1994

BELOVED HUSBAND   BELOVED WIFE

FATHER & GRANDFATHER   MOTHER & GRANDMOTHER

ת נ צ ב ה

The Israeli Steiners: (*L-R*) Avi, Yonah, Rivkah, Miriam, Shimone, Amit, Benjamin, and Liora Steiner, 2001 in New York City to celebrate David and Sylvia's eldest grandson, George Steiner's, bar mitzvah. (*Photgraph courtesy of Tamar Shavit and Shimon Rothstein.*)

(*L-R*) **Yonah and Rivkah Steiner, 2001.** (*Photgraph courtesy of Tamar Shavit and Shimon Rothstein.*)

The Holocaust memorial on Kibbutz Ginosar, built by Yonah Steiner to commemorate those Ginosar members' families who perished under the Nazis. Commanding the entrance of the kibbutz cemetery, the monument starts with a line of railroad tracks that leads to a broken Star of David, a cluster of chimney stacks, and finally to the sweet and peaceful waters of the Kinneret (Sea of Galilee).